AUTHOR YOUR AMBITION

THE COMPLETE SELF-PUBLISHING WORKBOOK FOR FIRST-TIME AUTHORS

M.K. WILLIAMS

ISBN: 978-1-952084-28-7 (Paperback)
978-1-952084-30-0 (PDF)
978-1-952084-29-4 (ePub)

Library of Congress Control Number: 2022919384

All content reflects our opinion at a given time and can change as time progresses. All information should be taken as an opinion and should not be misconstrued for professional or legal advice. The contents of this book are informational in nature and are not legal or tax advice, and the authors and publishers are not engaged in the provision of legal, tax, or any other advice.

Links included in this eBook might be affiliate links. If you purchase a product or service with the links that I provide I may receive a small commission. There is no additional charge to you, but it can help me continue to create and put out more content. Thank you for supporting my work so I can continue to provide you with helpful content!

Printed by M.K. Williams Publishing, LLC in the United States of America.
Cover Design & Interior Formatting by Formatted Books

First printing edition 2022.

authoryourambition@gmail.com
www.authoryourambition.com

This workbook is dedicated to JMW and CJW –
Thank you for your dedication to my dream. It allows me to dedicate my time to the authors who will use this workbook and their dreams.

Works by M.K. Williams

Non-Fiction
Self-Publishing for the First-Time Author
Book Marketing for the First-Time Author
How to Write Your First Novel: A Guide for Aspiring Fiction Authors
Going Wide: Self-Publishing Your Books Outside The Amazon Ecosystem

Fiction
The Project Collusion Series
Nailbiters
Architects

The Feminina Series
The Infinite-Infinite
The Alpha-Nina

Other Fiction
The Games You Cannot Win
Escaping Avila Chase
Enemies of Peace
Interview with a #Vanlifer

CONTENTS

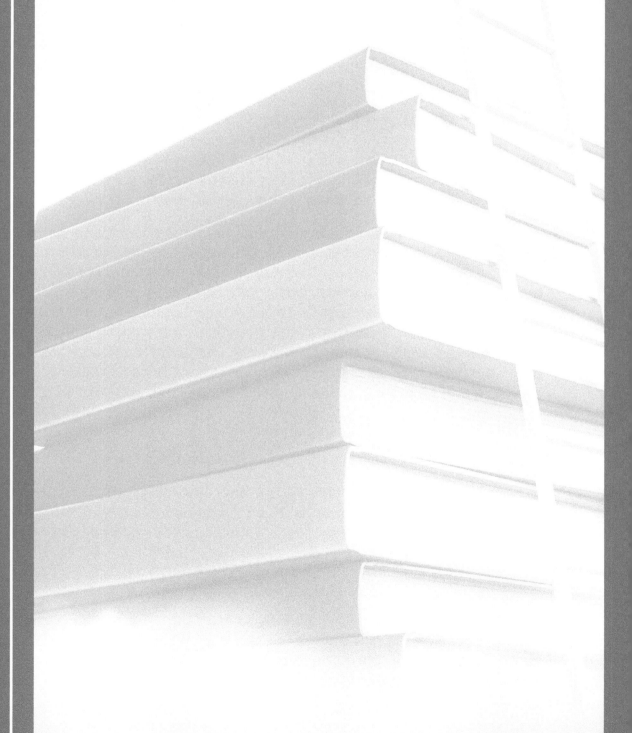

INTRODUCTION

I am a checklist person. Grocery lists. Task lists. Packing lists for vacations. Sometimes I'll get something done around the house and add it to my chores checklist so that I can cross it off. Hello, dopamine! I like a good list. Who doesn't like the feeling of crossing off everything on a to-do list, seeing everything done? It feels so good.

It is no surprise that I began creating a checklist when self-publishing my first book in 2015. My list grew with each book I published, and each client I helped to do the same. And grew. And grew.

It soon became what I called my "Mack Daddy" checklist. *This ain't your grandma's checklist.* I meticulously covered every step I needed to remember for my next book so I wouldn't lose any detail. I wanted my brain free to focus on the writing and creative part, not worrying if I missed a step or timing for any process.

As I began to take on more clients to help them get their books across the finish line, I would take my extensive list, make a copy, and amend it based on their goals. Some clients just wanted a print workbook for their eCourse that students could purchase from their website. Some wanted their book to be available in all formats and on all retailers. And every possible combination in between.

As my life changed with the birth of my daughter, I had less time to take on new clients. But I didn't want to stop helping people. And people didn't stop asking for guidance. *If only there were some way that I could download my brain so people could learn from me without having to do one-on-one calls.* The Author Your Ambition brand was born. And with it, a series of guidebooks for first-time authors. But those books explained the strategic options; they covered big and small picture items. None of them tell someone exactly what to do. What steps to take in precise order. I created worksheets to accompany those books to walk authors through exercises and help them make and track those strategic decisions.

Great! Problem solved!

Until they started to ask for more. As in, they wanted *the checklist*.

But how could I get a multi-tiered online checklist into a format that could be printed and give everyone all the options they might need or want but that could conflict with one another? I went back to the drawing board and kept adding to my list.

And finally, the words you are now reading are the preamble to my checklist. This is it. This is *the checklist*.

But it's not just a series of words for you to check off. I have added exercises and prompts to help you make the decisions that will determine which tasks to even complete. **This book contains the sheets and exercises to help you write, edit, self-publish, and market your book**. I've poured out my brain into this workbook.

HOW TO USE THIS WORKBOOK

There are a lot of options when it comes to self-publishing your book. This is amazing, considering that it was almost impossible to self-publish at the turn of the century, given the prohibitive print costs and non-existent distribution options.

But the downside to so many options is that, well, there are too many options. How can one workbook possibly anticipate every potential choice you can make about your book?

 It can't. It's also why **I recommend that you read through the entire workbook before you start doing anything**. I know you're super excited to get your book published already. But how can you know where to begin without looking through your options first? This process will show you all the potential opportunities so you can be confident in your self-publishing plan.

It's like PEMDAS. You remember from grade school, right? Please Excuse My Dear Aunt Sally. Or, in actual math terms, the order of operations for equations: Parenthesis, Exponents, Multiply, Divide, Add, Subtract. PEMDAS. As with every math equation, there is an order of operations to self-publishing. Sure, you can go out of order, but don't expect to get the intended outcome.

As you read through each section, you'll notice immediately if something is not for you or the strategy you selected. Cross it out with a big X. Tear it out of the book. Whatever you need to do so you know to skip that page or pages. And as you will be getting rid of the pages you don't need; make a copy of the ones you do.

MARKETING

WRITING & EDITING

TECHNICAL SETUP & PUBLISHING

Also, not every checklist could be in the exact order you'll have to use it. For starters, you should be talking about your book and marketing it from the outset, but that section is later in this book. You'll decide on a distribution strategy and then have to reference it later when it comes to uploading.

I've based the majority of this workbook on my personal experience and those of the authors I've worked with. That means this workbook is based on my experience as a U.S. citizen, writing and publishing in the U.S. I've added notes for other countries and regions where feasible. Be sure to verify any country-specific information for your location.

I've included a glossary in the next section, but you may need to refer back to it throughout the book for any new terms or acronyms that aren't familiar to you yet. There are a lot of endemic terms when it comes to self-publishing. We're authors; we love our lingo!

Each list will detail what you need to do in the order it should be completed. When necessary, I will give a direction that a task should be completed on your **Publication Date** or at a time related to your Publication Date (ex. **+2 Days after**

Publication or **-6 Weeks before Publication)**. These items will be **bold**. You can add the dates specific to your book on those lines. (You will have access to blank monthly calendars to fill in with your specific deadlines and important dates on Pages 14-27)

For first-time authors reading through, you'll notice specific actions are in ***bolded italics***. These items are specific to tasks you will need to take the very first time around. For authors who have already self-published, you can disregard these tasks – you've already done this.

Regardless of age, one thing I see most authors struggle with is the technology involved with self-publishing. Yes, even the "born with a cellphone in their hands" Gen Z-ers. Technology has made self-publishing available to us, but it can feel complex. Some software programs can do it all, but learning to leverage all the bells and whistles can be a lot. Then there are the websites to upload to. They have glitches or delays. Sometimes web servers go down. At the beginning of each section, I will include a scale like the one below with a guide for how easy or difficult that task will be in terms of tech-savvy. If you know you are not tech-savvy, if websites break in your presence, look to hire some help for the more technically difficult areas. If you are a computer pro and can learn a new program without blinking, you should feel confident mastering those tasks.

TECH-SAVVY

how hard is this step?

hard – requires tech skills & patience!

easy – most every author can tackle on their own

Also, you should not use every single page. This is not a Bible or canonical text of every single thing you MUST do "or else." I've provided lists of best practices, but I don't know a single author who has had a "perfect book launch" where they did every single thing they planned. Life happens. Also, some of the lists in this workbook are based on your decisions. For example, you should not do a DIY and professional cover. Pick one option and proceed accordingly.

I've put these sheets in the best order I can, but each of us has a different way of processing information. Self-publishing is an art as much as it is a science. This workbook is organized in the best way possible to help you navigate the ins and outs. This isn't one of those magical enchanted books you read about – the pages won't move into place for you and your specific book strategy. Review it first and remove the pages that don't apply to you or your strategy.

In a way, this is a "choose your own adventure" book.

And with that, let's get going. You have a book to write and publish!

GLOSSARY

20BooksTo$50K (Strategy) – Craig Martelle first articulated this strategy and founded the associated Facebook group and annual conference. The idea is that if you want to make a living income as an author of about $50,000 a year, you need to publish at least 20 books. Ideally, these books are all in the same genre and perhaps in the same series.

Aggregators – Self-publishing platforms that work with multiple retailers. You upload your book to that one platform, and they send it out to their network of retailers.

Alpha Reader – Someone who reads an early draft or even pages, whereas Beta Readers see a more developed manuscript. This is the very first person to read your manuscript or selected chapters.

Amazon Only (Strategy) – In the world of books, Amazon is King. Most authors want their books available for sale on Amazon. But some elect to ONLY have their book for sale on Amazon. This means their book is only available for sale on Amazon.com and/or Audible.com.

Author Copy – A copy of your book that looks exactly like a reader's copy. There are no markings on the book. You order the books at cost and can use them for marketing and promotions, to hand out, or to keep.

Bank over Rank (Strategy) – Wide distribution for your book also includes selling your book directly to readers. This can be from your website or at in-person events. Some authors worry that direct sales won't help their rankings or discoverability on retailers, especially Amazon.com. Well, some authors say, "Who cares? Take the sale!" The phrase "bank over rank" exemplifies this. If someone wants to buy your book right now, complete the sale and see that royalty in your bank account instead of worrying about your rank. Erin Wright, creator of the Wide for the Win Facebook group, first popularized this term.

Beta Reader – Those who have agreed to read your manuscript and provide critical feedback on what is unclear, what could be improved, and how.

Book Marketing Collateral – This can be anything that helps you to promote your book. From digital assets like social media images and posts to physical items like bookmarks and stickers. If you plan to attend book fairs or conferences, this could be your table decorations and any banners or signs. This is anything that helps you promote your book, not the book itself.

Book Metadata – This includes your book's title, subtitle, language, edition, series, description, categories, and keywords. Effectively, any pertinent information used to categorize or find your book.

Climax – This is it! The moment your story has been building towards. This is the battle royale that your character has been training for. This is when the detective in your novel reveals who committed the crime. This is the moment when your star-crossed lovers can finally be together.

Consignment – A method of selling where the retailer takes on no risk, and no one makes any money until the product sells. In the case of books, you would arrange to leave a few copies of your book at a local bookstore and agree on a consignment rate. When a customer purchases your book, both you and the bookstore make a cut from the sale. The financial risk is with the author in this case as they have already ordered copies of their book.

Cost-Per-Acquisition (CPA) – Some ads may charge a cost-per-acquisition, which is the best option. You only pay when you make a sale. But it can be hard to track this. You will likely calculate this on the back end.

Cost-Per-Click (CPC) or Pay-Per-Click (PPC) – Most of your advertising options with Amazon, BookBub, or Google are cost-per-click. Your ad will run, and many people will see it, but you will only pay when they click on it. (An ad that charges for views or impressions is on a CPM basis.)

Critique Group – A set of authors who agree to exchange chapters on a planned rotation. This allows each author to get multiple perspectives on what is or is not working in their book. Usually, one chapter is submitted ahead of an agreed-upon deadline, and feedback is sent back before a group call. This can provide accountability for the entire group.

Critique Partner – An author that you work with throughout the drafting process or after your first draft is completed. Usually, the two authors will exchange chapters and offer feedback on how they can be improved. Reviewing multiple chapters or the entire book may provide big-picture insights on character development, plot holes, and any structural improvements. This is a one-to-one relationship.

Direct Platforms – Have a one-to-one relationship with the retailer. As an example, Amazon KDP will self-publish your book to Amazon.com. Barnes & Noble Press will self-publish your book to BarnesandNoble.com.

Edit (Audiobook) – This is the phase when recorded audiobook files are cleaned up. Coughs. Rustling paper. The ten times you flubbed the same line over and over. All those little mess-ups are removed in this phase. You complete editing when you have one MP4 file for each chapter of your book.

Editorial Letter – An overarching review of the book and how it can be improved. This letter is usually provided with any developmental or story edits. While specific comments or suggested revisions may be noted within the manuscript itself, the editorial letter offers a big-picture overview of what is and is not working in the book and provides suggestions for how the author may correct some of those structural issues.

Formats – How your reader will consume your book (i.e., eBook, print book, audiobook).

Inciting Incident –The definition may be self-evident, but this is the event that kicks off your whole story. Some authors may choose to start their story with this incident from the get-go. Bam! Page one. Others may set the scene and introduce at least one or two characters and the setting before this event. Only you can know what is best for your book. But you can't leave the audience hanging for too long.

Kindle Select/Kindle Unlimited – Kindle Unlimited is a subscription offered by Amazon.com. It allows members to download and read unlimited books each month, so long as those books are enrolled in the program. Authors are compensated by the number of pages read; the royalties are pooled from the Kindle Unlimited membership fees. However, when an author enrolls in Kindle Select (which is how their book is included in Kindle Unlimited), they must list their eBook exclusively with Amazon. They are not permitted to have their eBooks listed on any other retailer – they can still have their print books or audiobooks on other retailers).

Launch – This is a marketing term related to introducing and promoting a new product, in this case: your book.

Launch Period – When you are promoting the book's release. If you aren't doing a pre-order, your launch period is the day you announce the book is for sale and the following weeks. If you will have a pre-order for your book, your launch period is the day you announce the pre-order through publication and the following weeks.

Master (Audiobook) – This is the phase when your edited MP4 files are polished. If you record a chapter in two settings, you will balance out the volume and ensure the decibels don't peak too high. You don't want your listeners to jump if it gets too loud too quickly. In this phase, you will ensure each file meets the requirements for uploading and submitting.

More Books Sell More Books (Strategy) – This concept generally means that the best way to sell more books is to write and publish more. As you have a more extensive backlist, you have more options for potential readers. It gives you credibility, and if you are writing in a series, it provides readers with a binge-able experience. If a reader had a positive experience with their first read, there's a good chance they'll research what other books you've published.

Offset Print – Most traditional publishers work with offset printers. They are ordering thousands of books to distribute to bookstores upon publication date. These books can be stored and warehoused while the book is on pre-order or as the publisher waits for more orders. The print cost is paid upfront, and the publisher knows they have to sell a certain number of books to cover the cost of printing and warehousing.

One Platform Only (Strategy) – This is when an author elects only to use one self-publishing platform to distribute their books. They may not have their book with every retailer, but they opt for simplicity over expanding their distribution.

Platforms – The sites where you will upload your book and manage all the book details. From here, the book data will filter to the retailer and become available to the reader.

Pre-Order – This is when the book is available on the major retailers for order, but the actual content is held until your publication date. This allows people to purchase now and get the book later. They have already paid, so on the book's "birthday," it will get to them as quickly as possible.

Print-on-Demand – This printing method allows self-publishers to offer print books without worrying about paying out of pocket for printing or warehousing. The print files are approved with the platform, and when a reader orders a book, they are printed and mailed to them. There is a slightly higher cost per book because the author cannot realize economies of scale with this method, but they also do not have to invest in significant capital upfront.

Proof Copy – A copy of the book ordered in the final editing phase and used as a last proofread. The expectation is that you would mark this up and address any final edits and tweaks BEFORE book publication. With Amazon KDP, when you order a proof copy, there is a gray band around the book that reads "PROOF COPY NOT FOR RESALE." With IngramSpark, your proof copy will not have this.

Publication Date – This is the "birthday" for your book. This is the date the book is published to the world and available to purchase immediately. For an eBook, the reader can start reading within seconds; for a print book, the order will process and get to the reader as quickly as their shipping selection allows.

Rapid Release (Strategy) – This strategy involves writing and releasing four or more books a year. Some say that two books in a year is Rapid Release. Given the amount of work that goes into each book, I agree. Usually, these books are all part of a series, and one is available for pre-order as soon as the previous one is published.

Reader Magnet – This is a marketing term for any content you create that can draw a reader in. This can be a free worksheet or video, or perhaps it is a side story or character origin story. Ultimately, this content introduces new readers to your writing to get them to read more of your work. You want to ensure you are asking for an email subscription in exchange for this free content so you can deliver this content and follow up afterward with a reminder to check out the associated book or series.

Record (Audiobook) – When you elect to narrate your own audiobook, the recording phase is when you sit down (in a quiet place with no ambient noise), hit record, and start narrating the book. This phase can be taxing on your voice, so stay hydrated and take breaks often. This will give your voice a rest and help you keep your energy up while narrating.

Reflowable – A "reflowable" eBook adjusts to the screen size the reader is viewing your book. The bigger the screen, the more words on a page. Automatically, like magic or computer code.

Resolution – This should be a relatively short section to close out the story. Now that the problem has been solved, the criminal brought to justice, and the world set right, it is time to wrap up any loose ends. This is where you can give your characters their happily ever after. Or, you can plant the seeds for a sequel. It is typically the final chapter of your book.

Retail Discount – This is the discount the store can apply to your book to help it sell. Depending on what they need to move, they may lump your book in with others for a 20% off sale or Hardcover sale. This discount should not affect the royalty you make from the sale.

Retailers – Where the reader will purchase your book.

Return on Ad Spend (ROAS) – This is your ROI. How profitable are these ads? Are you breaking even? Are you spending multiples of your royalty on one sale? You may be able to tolerate a poor ROAS if you are starting out and optimizing or trying to get people to start your series. But a negative ROAS means you are not earning back what you spend on ads.

Returnability – Most brick-and-mortar stores want to know that any products they sell can be returned to the producer if they cannot sell. This means the store is not on the hook to keep trying to sell something that isn't moving.

Rising Action – This portion of the book is where your characters get going. The incident has occurred, and now they have to take action. They have to go on a journey. They have to work together. They have to solve the mystery. This is going to be the longest portion of your story. The rising action exposes the clues, the journey twists and turns, and the character is challenged. This is the meat of the story. As the name implies, the stakes should get higher with each new chapter or scene. Throughout this section of your book, you want to be building towards the big reveal or challenge. In subtle ways, you'll need to remind the audience of the stakes involved for your character(s) throughout the story. Remind them why they are on this quest. Why don't they say, "eh, this is kind of hard. I'll just have a sandwich instead."

Royalty – The payment an author receives for their book sales.

Wholesale Discount – This is the discount you, as the author, offer to retailers to get them to stock your book. If the store pays the retail price for your book and then sells it at that same price, they actually lose money on the sale. They need a discount when purchasing the book so they can create margin. Most brick-and-mortar stores want to see a 50-55% wholesale discount.

Wide Distribution (Strategy) – Wide Distribution is the opposite of Amazon Only. Or any "one retailer only" strategy. It means that your books are available on multiple retailers. For some authors, wide means every possible retailer. For others, it means a handful. While self-publishing authors have been doing this for a while, Erin Wright coined the phrase and created a thriving social community known as "Wide for the Win."

Acronyms

ARC /ALC – Advance Reader Copy/Advance Listener Copy. A book copy provided to readers or reviewers before the publication date.

ACX – Audiobook Creation Exchange. This is Amazon's self-publishing platform for audiobooks. You can distribute your audiobook to Audible.com, Amazon.com, and Apple.com via this platform.

D2D – Draft2Digital. This self-publishing aggregator offers wide eBook and print distribution for your books. They acquired Smashwords in 2022, so this company is often referred to as Draft2Digital/Smashwords.

FV – Findaway Voices. This self-publishing aggregator specializes in audiobooks. They have an extensive distribution network and a marketplace to find narrators for your book.

IS – IngramSpark. This self-publishing aggregator allows you to publish your book on its massive distribution network.

ISBN – International Standard Book Number. This is the social-security number for your book, it uniquely identifies the title and format of your book.

KDP – Kindle Direct Publishing. This self-publishing platform allows you to publish your book on Amazon.com (and the associated country domains like .co. uk, .ca, .au, etc.)

KU – Kindle Unlimited. This subscription service allows members to read as many books in this program as they want in a given month. They are power-readers. They can still buy books on Amazon. Many look to maximize their subscription and read books in this program. Authors elect to join this program when uploading to KDP.

LCCN – Library of Congress Control Number. This is a registration number that will uniquely identify your book within the U.S. Library of Congress.

WIP – Work In Progress. A quick author shorthand for the book you are writing, editing, or working on right now.

BEFORE YOU GET STARTED

Let's get a few things clear. This workbook and its checklists are intended to help authors self-publish their books. If you want to get a traditional publishing deal, best of luck. This guide will not help you with that goal. If you are unsure which route to take, understanding the self-publishing process can assist you in making a decision.

Self-publishing is the action of taking on the responsibility to write, publish, and market a book under your own name (or selected pen name). You are the writer, the publisher, and the head of editorial and P.R. You are in charge of it all. It can be a power trip; it can also be overwhelming. Before diving in, let's make sure you have the right mindset:

1. **<u>Do you REALLY want to self-publish?</u>**

   Yes   No

Or do you see this as your second option since you didn't get a traditional deal? Know yourself. If you think this is just your "back-up option," you will self-sabotage. And by that, I mean at every step in the journey, you will stall, delay, wait, submit your book again, get frustrated, and generally not get the book published. If you are not sold on self-publishing, put this book down and do some soul searching. Are you ready to embark on this journey, or are you operating from a place of wounded pride over your last query rejection? If a traditional publishing deal is your actual aim, pause, regroup, and go back. At some point, you may decide self-publishing is the route to pursue. This workbook will still be here when you are ready to self-publish.

This isn't to deter you from self-publishing. This process is a commitment, and there will be challenges and mental hurdles. Having this commitment will help you complete the process and get your book out to your future readers.

Why do you want to self-publish this book? *What has led you to this decision? Write out your "why" here. When the going gets tough, it will be helpful to look back on your own words to inspire you to keep going:*

_____

_____

_____

_____

_____

2. **Who is on your side?** *They aren't signing a contract or committing to anything yet, but who are the people you know you can count on to cheer you on? Who is going to encourage you to keep going? Who will provide emotional support when the going gets tough?*

_____   _____   _____   _____

_____   _____   _____   _____

While I rattled off a bunch of items you were in charge of earlier, self-publishing is not solo-publishing. It is not solitary publishing. Accountability and encouragement from friends, family, and loved ones are critical to success. It would help if you had someone in your corner. This is a long process. It doesn't happen overnight; while you are writing and publishing this book, your life is still going on. Work stress, family problems, and car repairs can and will happen. Life can derail you. Having a support person to encourage you helps. And if you don't feel you have a friend to support you or a family member or partner to cheer you on, guess what? Welcome to the indie author community. We love that you are here, and we can't wait to cheer for you every step of the way.

3. **Outsource Something**

It's challenging to be a one-person publishing house. While you have your support team who keep you going, they may not be qualified to do any book-related work for you. You know which areas are your weak spots. Hire someone to design your cover, format your book, or coach you through the process. You can learn everything the hard and lonely way, or you can pay for assistance. I'll go over budgeting and costs later. But at the outset, have it in your mind that SOMETHING has to be done by someone else. I slogged through for years, trying to do it alone. It was so isolating and challenging when it didn't have to be.

If your weaknesses are... then... (circle the areas you know you can improve on)

- Grammar and punctuation -> Use a writing software and/or hire a copy editor
- Elements of Fiction (character, setting, plot, etc.) development -> Read craft books and/or hire a story editor
- Captivating creative non-fiction -> Read the best non-fiction books and/or work with a developmental editor
- Visual design of any kind -> Hire a cover artist and/or interior formatter
- Technology -> Review YouTube tutorials and/or hire a Book Consultant or Coach
- Social Media -> Take a course and/or talk to other authors in your position

MY TEAM

Now that you have thought about who will support you emotionally and who you might need to hire out, this is where you will list out your dream team. You likely won't assemble them all at once. You'll look to hire someone as the need arises. Or you may elect to truly do it on your own to save as much as possible. We'll cover price comparisons, budgeting, questions to ask, and more in the following sections. In subsequent sections, we'll also cover how to find various editors, formatters, etc. As you add someone to your team, refer to this page to enter their information to have all contact information in one place.

My Support Team

Name	Email Address	Phone Number
_____	_____	_____
_____	_____	_____
_____	_____	_____
_____	_____	_____

Editorial Team

	Name	Email Address
Developmental or Story Editor	_____	
Copy Editor 1	_____	
Copy Editor 2	_____	
Proofreaders	_____	
	_____	
	_____	
	_____	

Non-Professional Support – Critique Partners, Alpha Readers, Beta Readers

Refer to the glossary to see the distinction between these three types of readers. Remember that you may only need one or two of these readers as part of your editing process. **You don't need to have ALL these readers lined up. If you do, you might spend forever editing and never get the book published.**

Critique Partner(s)

Name	Email Address	Phone Number

Alpha Readers

Name	Email Address	Phone Number

Beta Readers

Name	Email Address	Phone Number

Design Team   Name   Email Address

Cover Design   _____

Illustrator (if applicable)   _____

Book Formatting   _____

Book Marketing Collateral   _____

ARC (Advance Review Copy) Readers & ALC (Advance Listening Copy) Listeners

Name   Email Address

_____

_____

_____

_____

_____

_____

Street Team (Your hype squad who did not sign on to be an ARC Reader/ALC Listener)

Name   Email Address

_____

_____

_____

_____

_____

_____

PERMISSION GRANTED

Along the self-publishing journey, you will face the ugly monster of doubt. "Who am I to write a book, let alone publish it?" "What gives me the right to create a story and put it out to the world?" "What if people don't like it, and all I get is criticism?" We've all had those doubts, but let me tell you – that ugly doubt monster is actually a tiny Pomeranian in an oversized costume. All bark and no bite.

It doesn't make those thoughts and worries any less real or paralyzing at the moment. So, to ease your fears, I am giving you permission. When you question yourself and think, "who gave me the permission to just do this?" answer yourself: "M.K. did!" You gave yourself that permission, but I've got you covered if you need it in writing.

In the following pages, you will find permission slips you can take out and date. Hang them next to your computer. Put them on your fridge. Place them in your notebook so you can easily reference them.

You have permission to:

- Write your book (be it fiction, non-fiction, or some experimental hybrid that has never been seen before)
- Self-publish that book
- Promote your book
- Hire someone to help you with your book
- Ask for a review for your book
- Ignore doubters and haters you encounter along the way

And most importantly...

- Take a break from all things book related

PERMISSION
TO WRITE YOUR NOVEL

GRANTED TO

That's right, you have permission to tell the story in your heart and in your mind. Only you can tell it. Only you can do it justice. In fact, you MUST write this book.

_____
Signature

_____
Date

PERMISSION
TO WRITE YOUR BOOK

GRANTED TO

That's right, you have permission to share the knowledge and expertise in your non-fiction book. Only you can tell it. Only you can do it justice. In fact, you MUST write this book.

_____
Signature

_____
Date

PERMISSION
TO SELF-PUBLISH

GRANTED TO

This book isn't going to publish itself. Without you to champion your words and get it out to the people, how else can people read your work? You have permission to self-publish your book the way that you see fit and that will bring your vision to life.

_____
Signature

_____
Date

PERMISSION
TO PROMOTE YOUR BOOK

GRANTED TO

No one will know about your book unless you tell them. And it is a great book, they should hear about it. They will be so happy that you told them about it once they have read it cover to cover. You just need to get the word out first!

Signature

Date

PERMISSION
TO HIRE SOMEONE TO HELP YOU

GRANTED TO

No one can do it all by themselves. It is okay to ask for help and to invest in your book. Bringing in a professional can help your book to succeed. Do your research and pick where your dollars go based on what help you need the most.

Signature

Date

PERMISSION
TO ASK FOR A REVIEW

GRANTED TO

Reviews don't just help you. They help the next reader know if your book is right for them. When you ask someone to leave a review for your book, you are really asking them to help the next person. These reviews help more people discover your book. That is a good thing and it doesn't take that long to do.

Signature

Date

PERMISSION

IGNORE THE DOUBTERS AND THE HATERS

GRANTED TO

"Pay no attention to what the critics say. A statue has never been erected in honor of a critic."

-Jean Sibelius

Signature

Date

PERMISSION

TO TAKE A BREAK FROM ALL THINGS BOOK-RELATED

GRANTED TO

Before you began this journey you were a person with a life, family, friends, and a job. That person still needs to rest. That person still needs to catch up with those who mean the most to them. Your book will be here tomorrow or next week (or next month). Rest and refill your creative well.

_____
Signature

_____
Date

DEFINE YOUR VISION AND GOALS

TECH-SAVVY

how hard is this step?

hard – requires tech skills
& patience!

easy – most every author
can tackle on their own

VISION

Before diving in and deciding HOW you will self-publish your book, you first need to have a clear vision and set of goals for your book. I've seen it happen too many times. An author starts out, and they hear about this "sure-fire" strategy, so they go with that, only to discover a totally different approach halfway in. Time is wasted. Money is burned. And books are delayed because of it.

I'll say this multiple times in the workbook and often say it aloud to authors in the real world, too: **there is no one right strategy for self-publishing. But there is a right path for you and your book**. We each have different goals and hopes for our books. We can't waste time copying what someone else did. And we can't know what is right for us until we spell out precisely what outcome we want from our books.

So, let's start with your vision. You likely already have this in your mind.

When you think of self-publishing your book, you see – what? Use this space to fill in what comes to mind. This can be how your book is received, where it is sold, and who reads it. Anything. What do you see? I'm intentionally not providing you with examples because I see it all too often. You'll see one and think, "yeah, that's what I want. And that too. And that too." Without any prompting from me, what is YOUR vision?

_____

_____

_____

_____

_____

_____

_____

_____

If you are struggling to come up with a vision from your point of view as the author, let's look at it from the other side: How will your story impact or help your readers?

_____

_____

_____

_____

_____

_____

_____

_____

Why are you writing this story, and what do you hope to achieve?

_____

_____

_____

_____

_____

_____

_____

_____

_____

GOAL

Now that you have the vision in mind, let's tackle HOW we can make that happen. We need to walk back and settle on what our goals will be. Let's break down the specific elements of your vision, whether it is the retailers you see your book in, the publication timeline, or the people who can read it. For example, if your vision is that your book inspires the next generation of readers, then your goal is to reach an audience within X age range.

ELEMENTS OF MY VISION

_____   _____   _____

_____   _____   _____

_____   _____   _____

_____   _____   _____

_____   _____   _____

_____   _____   _____

_____   _____   _____

_____   _____   _____

Of these elements, let's highlight the most important one. You can have multiple goals for your book and what it enables you to be. But one has to be the primary goal. When you have to decide to help one goal and possibly hinder another, you need to know which one takes priority. Let's rank these items:

#1 Priority Goal: _____

#2 Priority Goal: _____

#3 Priority Goal: _____

#4 Priority Goal: _____

If you only have two or three goals, that is fine! Don't feel like you need to add more on.

Additional goals that I will aim for, but won't take priority over my top listed goals:

_____   _____   _____

_____   _____   _____

_____   _____   _____

You've probably heard that goals need to be specific and measurable. You must define the exact parameters to know if you have reached that goal. "Lots of people read my book" is vague. To you, "lots" could be hundreds or thousands. Let's get specific so that you know when you have reached or even exceeded your goals.

#1 Priority Goal: _____

HOW WILL I KNOW WHEN GOAL IS MET?

_____

_____

_____

#2 Priority Goal: _____

HOW WILL I KNOW WHEN GOAL IS MET?

_____

_____

_____

#3 Priority Goal: _____

HOW WILL I KNOW WHEN GOAL IS MET?

_____

_____

_____

#4 Priority Goal: _____

HOW WILL I KNOW WHEN GOAL IS MET? _____

_____

_____

_____

Therefore, "my book will be successful if..."

_____

_____

_____

_____

_____

_____

_____

_____

_____

_____

_____

_____

_____

_____

_____

_____

And now for the crushing reality. I mean, planning for all contingencies. Let's start our plan with success in mind. That means we need to identify any obstacles or challenges.

What will be your biggest challenge(s) in writing this book and achieving your stated goals? How can you start to counteract this obstacle? For each challenge, provide a remedy to overcome it as best as possible.

_____

_____

_____

_____

_____

_____

_____

_____

_____

_____

_____

_____

_____

_____

_____

_____

_____

_____

_____

Now that we have explored what you see for the finished product, your end goals, and how to mitigate what will get in your way, let's start back at the beginning. (If you've already begun to write your book, enter today's date for the start date.)

Start Date: _____

Draft 1 Completed Date: _____

Ideal Publication Date*: _____

Final Word Count Goal: _____

Total Days to Write: _____

Daily Word Count Goal: _____

Unsure of the publication date, word count, etc.? Don't worry; we'll cover that later.

*Most authors take ten months to a year from first draft completion to ideal publication date.

TYPES OF GOALS:

Interim Deadlines: Your Draft 1 Completion Date and Publication Date are specific dates you are setting to reach the goal. You may miss your end deadline if you only put the publication date goal but don't know when the interim steps need to be done.

Word Count Goals: Not every author operates best under this method, but it is one way to track your progress. You can look up the average final word count for books in your genre and keep that in mind. You don't have to hit that word count exactly, but you can use it as a guide.

Stretch Goals: When you set short- and long-term goals, make them realistic. Can you get all of that work done in that amount of time? Be honest with yourself. But it can help to set a stretch goal too. I think I can get the first draft done by X date, but if I get it done a week earlier, I'll treat myself to...

BUDGET

TECH-SAVVY

how hard is this step?

hard - requires tech skills
& patience!

easy - most every author
can tackle on their own

You may have heard how much other authors have spent on different elements of their books. It can be expensive, but you can also be thrifty without sacrificing quality. In this section, we are going to go over your budgets.

Yes, multiple. Because you need to budget more than just the money you invest in your book. You have two other very expensive items to budget: your time and effort. That's right. Your time and effort are the most costly because you don't get it back once spent. You can always go out and find a way to earn more money to invest in your book. But you won't get any wasted hours back. You won't get the effort spent on a dead-end strategy returned to you.

Let's start with your time.

TIME

Writing a book takes time. Editing it takes even longer. When you get to the back of this workbook and are ready to hit "publish," you will be "so sick of this stinking book already." And that's perfectly natural!

But before we get to that point, the writing must get done. The book work has to happen.

When will you get your book work done? What is your dedicated time?

❏ Monday @ _____

❏ Tuesday @ _____

❏ Wednesday @ _____

❏ Thursday @ _____

❏ Friday @ _____

❏ Saturday @ _____

❏ Sunday @ _____

Select the days and times that currently work for you.

No time? Let's start to see what we can move around to make the time. It may take some temporary inconveniences to publish your book. But your work and effort will be worth it when you can hold your finished book in your hand. It is well worth the sacrifices to achieve this goal. Can you get up early two days a week to write? Can you skip your favorite shows for the next few months and then binge them once your draft is done? Can someone help watch the kids on weekend mornings? Let's get creative.

_____

_____

_____

_____

Next, we will look at the bigger timeline. While the book work is done on a regular basis each day or week, the whole book project comes together over months (sometimes years).

Self-Publishing Process   GANTT CHART

TASKS	MONTHS 1-3	MONTHS 4-6	MONTHS 7-9	MONTHS 10-12
Marketing				
Writing				
Editing				
Technical Set-Up				
Design				
Uploading				
Publication Prep				

The different elements of this workbook are represented on the above Gantt Chart so you can visualize how the process unfolds over time.

But this is a general timeline. You want to know what YOUR timeline will look like.

Let's keep track of our goal dates on the following calendar pages. This is also where you can fill in any significant dates in your personal life that you want to reserve for no work. Is there a trip that you need to consider in your planning? Will summer break mean less time to work on your book? Add those items to get a better picture of a realistic timeline for your book.

In the following 14 pages, you will find blank calendars. Each page represents one month. Fill them in with your planned deadlines for finishing your draft, sending your manuscript for editing, concepts back from your cover designer, your publication date, and so much more. Refer to these calendar pages as you work through this book, and add in deadlines as they are set. These are for you to see how many days, weeks, and months you have to work on your book.

When I work with first-time authors, from the very first step, the first idea for a book, I would say it takes about 12-14 months to complete the book. If they come to me after the first draft is done, maybe six to nine months. If they have all the editing done and are focused on the cover, formatting, and publication, then three to four months. The amount of time (and calendar sheets) you will need depends on where you are in the process.

Use what you need, and leave the rest.

MONTH: _____

SUN	MON	TUE	WED	THU	FRI	SAT

MONTH: _____

SUN	MON	TUE	WED	THU	FRI	SAT

MONTH: _____

SUN	MON	TUE	WED	THU	FRI	SAT

MONTH: _____

SUN	MON	TUE	WED	THU	FRI	SAT

MONTH: _____

SUN	MON	TUE	WED	THU	FRI	SAT

MONTH: _____

SUN	MON	TUE	WED	THU	FRI	SAT

MONTH: _____

SUN	MON	TUE	WED	THU	FRI	SAT

MONTH: _____

SUN	MON	TUE	WED	THU	FRI	SAT

MONTH: _____

SUN	MON	TUE	WED	THU	FRI	SAT

MONTH: _____

SUN	MON	TUE	WED	THU	FRI	SAT

MONTH: _____

SUN	MON	TUE	WED	THU	FRI	SAT

MONTH: _____

SUN	MON	TUE	WED	THU	FRI	SAT

MONTH: _____

SUN	MON	TUE	WED	THU	FRI	SAT

MONTH: _____

SUN	MON	TUE	WED	THU	FRI	SAT

EFFORT

Now that we know WHEN we will do the work let's figure out WHAT we are doing during that time. When I started, I had set times to write my book. But some days, the words just would not come. When that happened, I had a list of other "book work" to do. Going through this workbook is part of your book work. It will prepare you for when you get to the publishing phase. And once your book is published, you will have more book work to do.

Let's identify the different ways you can use your book work time:

Writing   Editing   Publishing   Optimizing   Marketing

Elements of my strategy to research (don't worry, after working through the next few sections this list will be full 😊)

_____

_____

_____

_____

_____

_____

_____

_____

_____

_____

_____

_____

MONEY

Now for the portion you've been looking forward to/secretly dreading. How much is all of this going to cost? Honestly, I can't tell you. Your budget will be completely different from mine and so many other authors. With some strategies, you can spend as little as $0 and, at the other end of the spectrum, as much as your credit limit allows. So much depends on your vision and genre and how thrifty/spendy you want to be. Yes, it will cost money. But you can find ways to save.

Below is a list of things you may (or may not) spend money on when self-publishing your book:

- Writing software
- Writing retreats
- Coffee or tea at a local café where you do your writing (at least you now have an excuse for the latte)
- Editing software
- Beta readers (some charge a fee)
- Thank-you gifts for Alpha and Beta readers
- ISBNs
- Copyright registrations
- Self-publishing platform upload fees
- Cover art & design
- Interior illustrations
- Book formatting software
- Book formatter
- Social Media Manager

- Pro level subscription to online design software
- Amazon Ads
- BookBub Ads
- BookBub Deals
- Facebook Ads
- Twitter Ads
- Instagram Ads
- TikTok Ads
- Ads Manager
- Paid newsletter swaps
- Paid review services
- Author copies of your books
- Promotional copies of your book (plus postage!)
- Marketing collateral (bookmarks, stickers, postcards)
- And so much more!

Let's start to build an ideal budget. How much do you think you can invest in your book? Maybe you don't have any extra cash to put into this. You can do this for free, but you will likely want to reinvest much of the royalties earned into optimizing and redoing things later. I was still trying to pay off my student loans when I started. So, I took gigs writing articles online for $20 a pop. I put that money into buying my

ISBNs and cover art for my first book. Get creative on how you can fund this project, and if something is too far out of your budget, remember that you can go back and release a new edition later with updated editing, formatting, and design. But as mentioned earlier, spending selectively can save you tremendous time, energy, and potential headaches.

Many of these elements are covered in the following sections, so you will want to refer back to this page later to input your planned costs.

It's always best to estimate on the high side, and hopefully, you come in lower and allow yourself to reinvest the remainder as new opportunities arrive. Use this budget to plan and sketch out what you think you will spend, and then you can mark your actual spend on the next page. This allows you to, hopefully, stay within your budget and can help you adjust expectations for future books.

Keep in mind that as you learn about each stage of the process and the potential costs that go with it, you may have no spend planned for several of these categories. That is perfectly fine. Mark a $0 (or you can make it a big ole happy face) and move to the next part.

You can claim a worksheet where you continue to edit and revise this budget at **AuthorYourAmbition.com/Budget**.

Phase	Service/Product	Planned Cost
Writing	Writing software	
	Writing retreats	
	Coffee or tea at a local café where you do your writing	
Editing	Editing software	
	Beta readers (some charge a fee)	
	Thank-you gifts for Alpha and Beta readers	
Technical Set Up	ISBNs	
	Copyright registrations	
	Self-publishing platform fees (IngramSpark, LuLu, PublishDrive)	
Design	Cover art & design	
	Interior illustrations	

	Book formatting software	
	Book formatter	
Marketing	Social Media Manager	
	Pro level subscription to online design software (Canva, BookBrush)	
	Amazon Ads	
	BookBub Ads	
	BookBub Deals	
	Facebook Ads	
	Twitter Ads	
	Instagram Ads	
	TikTok Ads	
	Ads manager	
	Paid newsletter swaps	
	Paid review services	
	Other paid book promotions	
	Author copies of your books	
	Promotional copies of your book (plus postage!)	
	Marketing collateral (bookmarks, stickers, postcards)	
Learning and Author Development	Professional Organizations (ex. SFF Writers, ALLi, RWA)	
	Writing Craft Courses and Webinars	
	Books on Craft or Author Business	
	Writing Masterminds	
	TOTAL:	

Price Ranges:

I'm providing a few examples of price ranges to help you start your budget. You can always adjust and change your estimates as you do your research.

- Writing Software: $60 Annual License or $250 Lifetime License or Google Docs is FREE
- Editing Software: $12 Monthly to $400 Lifetime
- Editors: $500-$5,000 depending on length, genre, and specialty
- ISBNs: $0-$125 per ISBN depending on your country
- Cover Art Design: $200-$4,000
- Illustrations: $100 per illustration to $10,000 for an entire book of illustrations
- Book Formatting: $150-$2,000 depending on the type of book and length

Actual Budget

Keep this page blank until you start to spend money on the book. Use this to track what you spend on the book to compare it to your plan. If you save in one area you can use that money elsewhere.

Phase	Service/Product	Actual Cost
Writing	Writing software	
	Writing retreats	
	Coffee or tea at a local café where you do your writing	
Editing	Editing software	
	Beta readers (some charge a fee)	
	Thank-you gifts for Alpha and Beta readers	
Technical Set Up	ISBNs	
	Copyright registrations	
	Self-publishing platform fees (IngramSpark, LuLu, PublishDrive)	
Design	Cover art & design	
	Interior illustrations	
	Book formatting software	
	Book formatter	
Marketing	Social Media Manager	
	Pro level subscription to online design software (Canva, BookBrush)	
	Amazon Ads	
	BookBub Ads	
	BookBub Deals	
	Facebook Ads	

	Twitter Ads	
	Instagram Ads	
	TikTok Ads	
	Ads manager	
	Paid newsletter swaps	
	Paid review services	
	Other paid book promotions	
	Author copies of your books	
	Promotional copies of your book (plus postage!)	
	Marketing collateral (bookmarks, stickers, postcards)	
Learning and Author Development	Professional Organizations (ex. SFF Writers, ALLi, RWA)	
	Writing Craft Courses and Webinars	
	Books on Craft or Author Business	
	Writing Masterminds	
	TOTAL:	

Once you know the total amount you have actually spent, you can start to determine your break-even point. Of course, your objective for publishing your book may not be profit maximization. While earning a profit is nice, you may just be happy to break even. You can skip this section if you aren't concerned about maximizing profits.

TOTAL ACTUAL SPEND: $_____

(From Page 35)

This chart may be best used in an Excel Document or Google Sheets. That way, you can edit the number of sales to see how much you *could* earn. I've created one that you can claim at **AuthorYourAmbition.com/Budget**

Also, the amount you earn on each sale will be slightly different. For starters, each platform offers somewhat different royalty rates for each sale. Some sales may be at a retail rate, others at a library rate. If you have a print book, the print cost also comes out of your cut. Ultimately you can drive yourself crazy trying to map it all out. But you can get a decent estimate of the earned royalty so you can plan how many books you'll have to sell to earn back your investment.

In the Resources section of this workbook, you will find links to the Estimated Royalty Calculator for the major self-publishing platforms. (Or you can do a quick search online for "[Platform Name] + Estimated Royalty Calculator" and find it that way too.)

How to know how many books you will sell? That's hard to tell. It can depend on the size of your audience, the gusto with which you post on social media, and the once-in-a-lifetime opportunity you have to chat with a mega-influencer. I suggest making a low, medium, and high range. What is your worst estimate? What is the best-case scenario? That can give you an idea of the range of what you could earn.

This exercise can also help you determine IF you will add a new format.

Royalty earned on a book * # books sold = Your Take

	Estimated Royalty Per Sale	X # of Sales	Subtotal
Royalty on eBook Sales			
Royalty on Paperback Sales			
Royalty on Hardcover Sales			
Royalty on Audiobook Sales			
		TOTAL ROYALTY:	

Breakeven Point:
TOTAL ROYALTY – TOTAL SPEND ≥ $0

Before we leave this section, I need to remind you of something:

Your book, goals, and vision are all unique to you. Your budget is the same way. Just because someone else spends thousands on their book doesn't mean you should blindly follow. **Spending additional money does not automatically guarantee best-seller status**. You know your budget, your risk tolerance, etc. You are the one who will look at the financials and have to reconcile the costs, not the person who told you to blow $10,000 on *insert audacious book-related item here.*

It's okay if one service is out of your price range. I guarantee you there is one that will be within your budget. Nowadays, there are service providers for every step of the self-publishing process to match every budget. Shop around and ask for recommendations.

There are vendor price comparison worksheets for you to complete throughout this workbook. Here you will be able to note the different service providers you research, what they offer, how quickly they can help you, and what it will cost. You'll find them in the appropriate section:

Vendor Price Comparison Worksheets

Developmental / Story Editor: Pages 136-138
Copy Editor: Pages 148-150
Cover Design: Pages 200- 202
Formatting: Pages 215-217

YOUR SELF-PUBLISHING STRATEGY

TECH-SAVVY

how hard is this step?

hard - requires tech skills
& patience!

easy - most every author
can tackle on their own

Most of the decisions and exercises in this section are sourced from my books: *Self-Publishing for the First-Time Author* and *Going Wide: Self-Publishing Your Books Outside the Amazon Ecosystem*. In the world of self-publishing, there are many different strategies. Some are popular and have catchy alliterative names and massive followings. Some are small and niche. This workbook will cover all essential/or mainstream strategies to get your book out to the masses. As you work through this book, you will see some larger overarching themes, and you can start to piece together what strategy will work for you. I'll define some of the largest ones here for you to reference and research:

More Books Sell More Books – This concept generally means that the best way to sell more books is to write and publish more. As you have a more extensive backlist, you have more options for potential readers. It gives you credibility, and if you are writing in a series, it provides readers with a binge-able experience. If a reader had a positive experience with their first read, there's a good chance they'll research what other books you've published.

> **20BooksTo$50K** – Craig Martelle first articulated this strategy and founded the associated Facebook group and annual conference. The idea is that if you want to make a living income as an author of about $50,000 a year, you need to publish at least 20 books. Ideally, these books are all in the same genre and perhaps in the same series. So, ten books do not necessarily translate to $25,000 a year in royalties. And if it takes you a year to write and publish a book, 20 books could take 20 years. Well, that is where Rapid Release comes in.

> **Rapid Release** – This strategy involves writing and releasing four or more books a year. Some say that two books in a year is Rapid Release. Given the amount of work that goes into each book, I agree. Usually, these books are all part of a series, and one is available for pre-order as soon as the previous one is published.

Amazon Only – In the world of books, Amazon is King. Most authors want their books available for sale on Amazon. But some elect to ONLY have their book for sale on Amazon. This means their book is only available for sale on Amazon.com and/or Audible.com. Why would they want that?

> **One Platform Only** – For starters, it can be a matter of simplicity. Having one retailer means only one set of reports, tax documents, and a very clear link to send readers to.

Kindle Select/Kindle Unlimited – Others are taking advantage of Amazon's marketing program, Kindle Select. This requires exclusivity for eBooks (meaning you are not permitted to have your eBooks listed on any other retailer – you can still have your print books or audiobooks on other retailers).

Wide Distribution – Wide Distribution is the opposite of Amazon Only. Or any "one retailer only" strategy. It means that your books are available on multiple retailers. For some authors, wide means every possible retailer. For others, it means a handful. While self-publishing authors have been doing this for a while, Erin Wright coined the phrase and created a thriving social community known as "Wide for the Win."

"Bank over Rank" – Wide distribution for your book also includes selling your book directly to readers. This can be from your website or at in-person events. Some authors worry that direct sales won't help their rankings or discoverability on retailers, especially Amazon. Well, some authors say, "Who cares? Take the sale!" The phrase "bank over rank" exemplifies this. If someone wants to buy your book right now, complete the sale and see that royalty in your bank account instead of worrying about your rank. Erin Wright, creator of the Wide for the Win Facebook group, first popularized this term.

M.K.'S STRATEGY

While I want you to focus on *your* book, *your* vision, and *your* goals, I know it can be helpful to see what others are doing. As I detail my strategy throughout this section, I hope you can find some inspiration on what will and won't work for you.

I follow a Wide Distribution strategy, and while I also abide by the idea that More Books Sell More Books, I do not have a Rapid Release schedule.

AMAZON ONLY OR WIDE SELF-PUBLISHING

Before we sink our teeth into the basics of your strategy (your formats, retailers, and platforms), we need to go over a significant decision for you as an author: will you be exclusive to Amazon? It's an essential question because Amazon KDP has its own set of rules to follow if you choose to be exclusive with Amazon. Amazon KDP (Kindle Direct Publishing) is the platform that will allow you to self-publish your book directly to the Amazon website.

Every author I have ever worked with asked, "how do I get my book onto Amazon.com?" It is a critical retailer for most products, especially books. You absolutely want to be there, and there are many different avenues you can use to get your book on Amazon.com and the associated country domains outside the United States (ex., co.uk, .au, .ca).

But do you ONLY want to be on Amazon? For me, I decided at the outset that I wanted to be in libraries. I also wanted people to access my book from whichever platform they were the most comfortable with. Other authors look for simplicity and pick just one retailer: Amazon. Or they look at the potential income from the Kindle Select Program (Page 58) and decide they would do better in that program than with all the other retailer royalties they are forgoing.

Only you know the right answer for your book and your strategy.

A few things to keep in mind:

- You can always go from "Amazon Exclusive" to "Wide" if you want to change your strategy. Going from "Wide" to "Amazon Exclusive" is much trickier.
- You should think on this decision, really think about it. Do your research on which genres do best in Kindle Select. Assess how much extra work you want to take on with each additional platform and retailer.
- You can have your eBook listed with Kindle Unlimited and only on Amazon, but have your print book and audiobooks listed wide. The decision can be made for each book and each format.

- There is no one correct answer that applies to all authors. Each book, each author has a unique plan and vision.
- This is a **strategy**. A bad month of sales on any one retailer shouldn't cause you to hit a panic button and switch. A poor sales trend after you have done everything to optimize your strategy would justify a change.
- At the most basic level, Amazon Only can be the easiest, quickest, and least expensive way to self-publish your book. However, you are limiting your customers who shop on other platforms, potential access to libraries, and ways to communicate directly with your readers (by selling direct).

I have multiple videos on this topic on my YouTube Channel. You can check this one out to help in your decision process: "Self-Publish Wide or Amazon Exclusive?"

YOUR STRATEGY

- ❏ Amazon Exclusive
- ❏ Wide

The upload checklists for each strategy can be found on:

Amazon Exclusive: Pages 236-239   Wide: Pages 240-253

We're heading into the weeds of decision-making for self-publishing at this point. Let's make decisions on:

1. **Formats** – how your reader will consume your book (i.e., eBook, print book, audiobook).
2. **Retailers** – where the reader will purchase your book.
3. **Platforms** – the sites where you will upload your book and manage all the book details. From here, the book data will filter to the retailer and become available to the reader.

FORMATS

Let's plan out how readers will interact with your book. How will they get to read it?

Here are the primary formats for you to consider and the different venues you'll have to publish in those formats:

- eBook
  - ePub
  - PDF/ editable PDF
- Print
  - Paperback
  - Hardcover
  - Large Print
- Audiobook
  - Digital files
  - Physical CDs

Here are the things to keep in mind and think about as you select your formats:

ePub is the most common file type for your eBook. Just as a .doc or .docx is your file type for Microsoft Word or .xls or .xlsx is the file type for Excel.

eBook

Save the Masterfile for your book in Microsoft Word 97-2003 .doc version. This format is preferred when uploading to Smashwords. And any time I've ever uploaded a Word doc to a platform like KDP or Smashwords, I got almost no error messages when it was a 97-2003 .doc; the .docx usually gives more issues.

Creating an ePub file takes some technical skill and know-how. You can't "save as" an ePub from a Word doc. You'll either need special software for writing (like Vellum or Scrivener) or to work with someone who can format and convert your file. Sometimes, you can upload your Word doc to the platforms, and they will convert it for you. Others require you to bring a converted file.

Have both an ePub and Mobi file for your **reflowable** eBook. (A "reflowable" eBook means that the text will adjust no matter what screen size the reader is viewing your book on. The bigger the screen, the more words on a page. Automatically, like magic or computer code.)

Amazon is phasing out the Mobi, but until it is entirely out of circulation, it is good to have it as a backup.

WHEN SHOULD YOUR BOOK BE AN EDITABLE PDF INSTEAD OF AN EPUB?

Is the intent of your book for the reader to be able to journal, complete exercises within the book, and fill out the pages?

If so, an editable PDF may be a better digital alternative to the print book than an ePub file.

If you are selling your eBook as a PDF – does it NEED to be an <u>editable</u> PDF for your audience?   ❏ Yes   ❏ No

Will you be exclusive to Amazon KDP?   ❏ Yes   ❏ No (See Page 60)

Will there be bonus content exclusive to this format? Authors often provide bonus content to incentivize readers to buy a specific format.

Reader Magnet – additional content readers can access when they subscribe to your email list.

> Is that something you want to offer? Or will you save any bonus content as a reader magnet?
> If you do bonus content for the eBook, how will you market that to the reader?

_____

_____

_____

_____

_____

_____

_____

_____

Within the print format, you have several options. You can have a paperback (softcover), a hardcover, or both. If you elect a hardcover, you can have a book with a dust jacket or just the case laminate cover. You will select these options from the self-publishing platforms when you upload. There are many different decisions – each one is broken down below for you to consider:

Print:

- No – Skip to Page 48
- Yes

  - Binding Type:
    - Paperback – Perfect Bound
    - Hardcover – Case Laminate
      - Dust Cover?
  - Trim Size: _____
    - Is that trim size available with all of your planned platforms? (Page 56)
    - Will you do the same trim size for both paperback and hardcover if you are doing both?
    - If no, you will need a separate print interior file for each.
  - Interior Color
    - Black & White
    - Full Color
  - Paper Type
    - White
    - Crème
    - Groundwood* only available via IngramSpark
  - Print Size
    - Regular
    - Large Print
    - Barcode (see Page 169)
    - Use free barcode from platform
    - Purchase barcode with price

TRIM SIZE

What size should you pick? Well, what size are the books in your genre? Review the books you want to compare to and look at their dimensions. (With a ruler or measuring tape. Or check the listing for those books online. They usually include the trim size.) Chances are you will want to be about that size as well.

Next, check the self-publishing platforms you will upload to and see if that size is available. If not, is there one that is close to that size? Check that all your planned platforms have that size available.

PAPER TYPE

Isn't paper just paper? Well, if you publish a book with lots of full-color images, you likely want premium paper, and you'll want it to be on white paper so that colors stay true.

If your book is primarily text, then you want a crème paper. This is less harsh on the reader's eyes.

A few things to keep in mind:

1. Even if you aren't planning on adding a hardcover format on launch, get the cover files. It makes it much easier to add it later than going back and having the cover design redone.
2. Color printing on the interior is for all pages. The entire book is printed in color, even if you have just one or two pages that need color. It is more expensive. So, how much do you really NEED those color images?
3. Some paper types (ex., Groundwood) are not available on all platforms.
4. Some trim sizes are not available on all platforms. Standard trim sizes like 5.5"x8.5", 6"x9", and 5"x8" are available across all platforms.

Will there be bonus content exclusive to this format?
Authors often provide bonus content to incentivize readers to buy a specific format.

> Is that something you want to offer?
> Or will you save any bonus content as a reader magnet?
> If you do bonus content for the print book, how will you make that clear to the reader?

_____

_____

_____

_____

_____

_____

Audiobook

Audio is quickly growing as a popular book format for listeners/readers. Authors are trying to keep up with demand. However, audiobooks are also the most labor-intensive (and expensive) format to produce. There is just more to do, and it all takes time – which isn't cheap. Here are some of the elements to consider and research. Remember, you can always add this format later.

First, do you want to have an audiobook format for your book?

Do you want readers to be able to access your book in audio?   ❑ Yes   ❑ No

Do you have the funds to invest in narration or the time to narrate and edit it yourself?   ❑ Yes   ❑ No

If you think this is something you want to explore or add on later, you can return to this section later. While it is great to launch all formats simultaneously, no rule says you have to. You can add the audiobook format next year (or even later.)

Audiobook:

- ❑ No – Skip to Page 50
- ❑ Yes

    - Who will narrate?
        - You!
            - Where will you record?
            - How will you learn Audacity (or another audio recording software)?
            - What gear do you already have? What do you need?
        - Professional Voice Actor(s)
            - What is your budget for narration?
            - Where will you find these actors?
                - ACX Marketplace
                - Findaway Voices Marketplace

- Recommendations from other authors
- Audiobook narrator forums
  - Will the voice actor provide mastered files or will they need to be edited?
- Artificial Intelligence/ Auto narration
  - What is your budget?
  - Will your selected platforms accept an A.I. narrated audiobook?
- Will you be exclusive to ACX or go wide? (Page 66)

A few things to keep in mind:

1. You will want to promote this format specifically in addition to your promotions for the book overall. You can use audio clips to help promote the book.
2. Your cover should have both the author and narrator listed.
3. For authors outside the U.S., U.K., Canada, and Ireland, you will not have access to ACX or their marketplace for narrators.

Will there be bonus content exclusive to this format?
Authors often provide bonus content to incentivize readers to buy a specific format.

We'll learn about ACX on Page 65, but for now:

1. ACX is Audiobook Creation Exchange. It is how you self-publish your audiobook directly to Audible and Amazon.com.
2. Regardless of your plan for an audiobook, once your eBook is available for sale on Amazon.com, you should claim it on ACX. Pirates out there claim books and sit on them or make money off work they didn't create. Scary, but the solution is easy. Claim your audiobook on ACX within 24 hours of it going live on Amazon.com as an eBook.

Is that something you want to offer?
Or will you save any bonus content as a reader magnet?
If you do bonus content for the audiobook, how will you make that clear to the reader?

_____

_____

_____

_____

_____

_____

_____

YOUR SELECTED FORMATS

Check the formats you will use for your book.

- ☐ eBook
  - ○ ePub
  - ○ PDF/ editable PDF

- ☐ Print
  - ○ Paperback
  - ○ Hardcover
  - ○ Large Print

- ☐ Audiobook
  - ○ Digital files
  - ○ Physical CDs

M.K.'S STRATEGY

My strategy involves having my books available in all possible formats. When I first began self-publishing in 2015, I had an eBook-only strategy that worked for me then. Now, I want all available formats to meet readers where they are and with what they want.

SECTION END:

After working through this section, you should have the following:

- ☐ Confirmed list of formats for your book.
- ☐ Clarity on what you will need to execute on each format. As we examine retailers and platforms in the following sections, we'll confirm which file types you need, file sizes, etc

RETAILERS

Before you decide which self-publishing platforms you will upload your book to, you will first need to define where your readers will purchase the book. Once we know the retailers, we can back into the publishing platforms. Below is a list of the major retailers where readers buy books. If one is missing from the list that you want to pursue, then add it and look up which platforms distribute to that retailer.

- ☐ Amazon.com (and associated domains: .co.uk, .au, .de, etc.)
- ☐ Barnes & Noble – Brick and Mortar local stores
- ☐ BarnesandNoble.com
- ☐ Kobo/Rakuten
- ☐ Target.com
- ☐ Walmart.com
- ☐ Apple Books
- ☐ Google Play Books
- ☐ Your local library
- ☐ Your local independent bookstore
- ☐ Bookshop.org
- ☐ Audible.com
- ☐ Audiobooks.com
- ☐ Chirp.com
- ☐ Your website
- ☐ _____
- ☐ _____
- ☐ _____
- ☐ _____

PLATFORMS

Now that we know the retailers let's back out and see which platforms can get you access to distribute to these retailers. This is not an exhaustive list, and as self-publishing platforms add new retailers to their list, it is an ever-changing landscape.

There are multiple ways to get to some of these retailers. In some cases, you'll have one clear option. For some retailers, you will have many different options.

You may wonder, "why not select EVERY option?" Depending on your strategy, that may work. Or you may want to keep it simple and only have one account, password, and tax form to manage. The number of platforms (and retailers) is entirely up to you.

First, look at the retailers you want your book to be sold with. Then cross-reference the platforms that can get you there. I encourage authors to be efficient with their platforms. Signing up for every single platform can cause duplicate listings and headaches. Ideally, you want a few platforms to get you all the retailers on your list.

I recommend you read this section in its entirety first, then go back with the information you have to select which platforms you will work with.

Retailers	Platforms	Direct					Aggregators					
		Amazon KDP	Barnes & Noble Press	Google Play Books	Apple Books for Authors	Kobo Writing Life	IngramSpark	Draft2Digital/Smashwords	LuLu	Audiobook Creation Exchange (ACX)	Findaway Voices	PublishDrive
Amazon.com		X					X	X	X	X	X	X
Barnes & Noble – Brick-and-mortar stores			X				X	X	X			
BarnesandNoble.com			X				X	X	X		X	
Kobo/Rakuten						X	X	X	X			X
Target.com							X					
Walmart.com							X				X	
Apple Books					X		X	X	X	X	X	X
Google Play Books				X				X			X	X
Your Local Library							X	X	X		X	X
Your Local Independent Bookstore							X	X	X			
Bookshop.org							X					
Audible.com										X	X	X
Audiobooks.com											X	
Chirp.com											X	
Scribd								X	X		X	X

As you can see, many different platforms can get your book on Amazon.com. Only a handful of platforms can get your book to Walmart.com or Target.com.

When it comes to self-publishing platforms, you can either go DIRECT or with an AGGREGATOR.

Direct platforms have a one-to-one relationship with the retailer. As an example, Amazon KDP will self-publish your book to Amazon.com. Barnes & Noble Press will self-publish your book to BarnesandNoble.com.

Aggregators work with multiple retailers. You upload your book to that one platform, and they send it to their network of retailers.

	PROS	CONS
Direct Platforms (Amazon KDP, Barnes & Noble Press, Google Play Books, Kobo Writing Life, Apple Books for Authors)	• You have more control over the book listing. • You get a higher royalty on each book sale. • One for one – you upload to that platform and the book shows up on that retailer's website.	• You ONLY get your book onto that retailer website. That's it. • These platforms exist to help the retail website sell more books. The primary focus is the customer, not the author. • If you have multiple direct retailers that is more work for uploading, updating, and maintaining your book. Not to mention all the passwords.
Aggregators (IngramSpark, Draft2Digital/Smashwords, LuLu, ACX, Findaway Voices)	• You upload once and your book goes out to multiple retailers. • The aggregators were made to help authors. • For some retailers this is your only avenue to get your book onto their platform.	• Slightly lower royalty since the aggregator gets a cut of each sale as well. • Less direct control over your listing. • Glitches on your book listing mean contacting BOTH the retailer and aggregator customer service. Pack your patience!

Using my books as an example. I've chosen to Go Wide.

My formats include:

- eBook
- Paperback
- Hardcover
- Audiobook

My Retailers include:

- Amazon.com (and associated domains: .co.uk, .au, .de, etc.)
- Barnes & Noble – Brick and Mortar local stores
- BarnesandNoble.com
- Kobo/Rakuten
- Target.com
- Walmart.com
- Apple Books
- Google Play Books
- Your local library
- Your local independent bookstore
- Bookshop.org
- Audible.com
- Audiobooks.com
- Chirp.com
- My website
- As many as possible!

In order to reach those Retailers, my platforms for uploading include:

- Amazon KDP
- Google Play Books
- IngramSpark
- Draft2Digital/Smashwords
- ACX
- Findaway Voices
- PayHip (direct sales from website)

Remember, this is my strategy. And I didn't use all these platforms for my first book. I started small and added more as I learned.

SELLING YOUR BOOK ON YOUR WEBSITE

Selling your book directly to readers from your website has many benefits. You can build a direct relationship with your audience and get to keep more royalties on each sale. Depending on your website host, tech-savvy expertise, and willingness to market this option, you may forgo direct sales or put it on the back burner. The e-commerce landscape is constantly evolving. Do some research and ask other authors you know about how they handle sales on their websites. Does their process sound easy? Give it a try! Sounds complicated? Then you can skip it. As noted above, I use PayHip to process direct sales on my website.

Which platforms kept popping up on your list? Select the platforms that will get you to the majority or all of your intended retailers.

- ❏ Amazon KDP
- ❏ Barnes & Noble Press
- ❏ Google Play Books
- ❏ Kobo Writing Life
- ❏ Apple Books for Authors
- ❏ IngramSpark
- ❏ Draft2Digital/Smashwords
- ❏ LuLu
- ❏ ACX
- ❏ Findaway Voices

For reference, these are the formats each platform will allow you to publish. As you look at your list, you may have several aggregators. If you are stuck deciding between several, look to see which one gets you the most coverage in terms of formats as well.

I have multiple videos on the different retailers on my YouTube Channel.

You can check out the different playlists I have for:

"Amazon KDP"

"IngramSpark"

"GooglePlay"

And many more!

Amazon KDP	IngramSpark	Draft2Digital/Smashwords	Barnes & Noble Press	Google Play Books
eBook Paperback Hardcover	eBook Paperback Hardcover	eBook Paperback **D2D Only	eBook Paperback Hardcover	eBook Audiobook **AI Auto narrated Only
LuLu	**Kobo Writing Life**	**Apple Books**	**ACX**	**Findaway Voices**
eBook Paperback Hardcover	eBook Audiobook	eBook Audiobook	Audiobook	Audiobook

Based on which retailers you selected, which platforms will get you into the most retailers? How many platforms do you want to manage logins and tax information for? This is something only you can answer.

Next, I will have platform-specific checklists based on the ones that fit your strategy. You will likely not use all of these, and you probably shouldn't either. I always recommend efficiency. Go direct with the retailers that make the most sense for you and your strategy, and then pick one aggregator for the rest. (**NOTE**: *Pages 58-66 are for first-time authors*. If you already have your accounts set up, then you can skip.)

⧗ When To Tackle

I suggest you have your platform strategy locked in as you work through your edits. You will have time while your book is with your editors to think about the strategy and adjust before you upload anything. If you wait until you have the finished document, you may not have everything you need (different platforms have slightly different file requirements). You also need to set up each account, which takes time. I always tell authors to use their downtime while the book is in editing or formatting to set up the necessary accounts.

Next are the checklists you will use when setting up your self-publishing platform accounts. We'll start with the direct platforms and then move to the aggregators. Only use the lists and create the accounts you need based on the exercise from Page 56. I recommend signing up for the platforms while your book is in formatting and design.

Amazon KDP

Amazon KDP or Kindle Direct Publishing allows you to self-publish your eBook, paperback, and/or hardcover books to Amazon.com and the associated territory domains.

Account Set-Up Checklist

- ☐ Create login at https://kdp.amazon.com/en_US/. (You will use your current personal Amazon.com login or you will need to create a new login for your author email address. Amazon is smart though and will know that the two accounts are associated, so you can't leave a review for your own book.)
- ☐ Input banking information for payment.
- ☐ Complete "tax interview" for end-of-year royalty tax purposes.
- ☐ Terms & Conditions accepted.

Kindle Select/Kindle Unlimited and Amazon Exclusivity

Before we go any further, we must go over a big strategy within self-publishing. Kindle Select is the KDP program that allows self-publishing authors to enroll their books in Kindle Unlimited.

Kindle Unlimited ("KU") is a subscription program that allows members to read as many eBooks as they want in the program. Readers pay a monthly subscription fee for this service. Authors are compensated from this pool of subscription fees based on the number of pages read. Write a page-turner and earn more. Write a dud and make less. It is very fair.

However, to enroll your eBook in this program, you must keep it exclusive to Amazon. That means your eBook cannot be sold on your website, available at your local library, or any other retailer. **This restriction only applies to your eBook.** You are still free to sell your paperback and hardcover anywhere, even while enrolled in Kindle Select.

Kindle Select is an option you can elect when you upload your eBook. The term of your enrollment is 90 days. You can remove your book from the program at any time, and at the end of the current 90-day span, you are free to publish the eBook elsewhere. While enrolled in this program, you can still sell your paperback and hardcover anywhere, and you can still sell your eBook to Amazon.com readers who do not have Kindle Unlimited. You can use countdown deals and free book promotions while enrolled in Kindle Select.

You can enroll your eBook in this program after publication as well. However, if you have already distributed your eBook wide, removing listings to comply with the exclusivity becomes a bit trickier. If you want to test out Kindle Select, I recommend trying it first. Then if it doesn't work, go wide, not the other way around.

The significant advantage is getting access to the "power users" who only read books via Kindle Unlimited; however, you limit your potential eBook sales to Amazon.com.

KDP defines Kindle Select as a Marketing Resource. However, your decision to be exclusive comes into play at this stage before you sign up for all the other platforms. Consider these factors when making your decision:

Does your genre appeal to Kindle Unlimited readers?
    ❏ Yes   ❏ No

Will you be writing in a series or a standalone book?
    ❏ Series ❏ Standalone

Will you make use of (and promote) a countdown deal?
    ❏ Yes   ❏ No

Will you make use of (and promote) a free book promotion?
    ❏ Yes   ❏ No

KINDLE SELECT FEATURES

When enrolled in Kindle Select, you can use the special marketing features: countdown deals and free book promotions.

To be clear, you can offer your book for free for a limited time or make it perma-free without being enrolled in Kindle Select. You can discount your book for a limited time, but you must manually change the price and market the deadline.

These features allow you to set these promotions and pre-schedule them without turning them off.

Based on the research you've done and your vision, will you enroll in Kindle Select and forgo self-publishing your eBook on other platforms?:

- ❏ Heck yes, sign me up for Kindle Select!
- ❏ No way, I'm going Wide!
- ❏ Eh, I want to try it out for the first 90 days and see from there.

Barnes & Noble Press allows you to self-publish your eBooks and print books directly to BarnesandNoble.com.

Account Set-Up Checklist

- ❐ Create login at https://press.barnesandnoble.com/create-account.
- ❐ Input banking information for payment.
- ❐ Complete tax information for end-of-year royalty tax purposes.
- ❐ Terms & Conditions accepted.

Google Play Books allows you to self-publish your eBooks directly to the Google Play Bookstore. In 2022 they added an auto-narrated audiobook feature utilizing A.I. (artificial intelligence). You can sell an audiobook on the platform so long as you have the eBook listed in the Google Play Bookstore.

Account Set-Up Checklist

- ❐ Create login at https://play.google.com/books/publish/u/0/.
- ❐ Input banking information for payment.
- ❐ Complete tax information for end-of-year royalty tax purposes.
- ❐ Terms & Conditions accepted.

Kobo Writing Life (KWL) allows you to self-publish your eBooks and audiobooks directly to their storefront.

Account Set-Up Checklist

- ❐ Create login at https://www.kobo.com/us/en/p/writinglife.
- ❐ Input banking information for payment.
- ❐ Complete tax information for end-of-year royalty tax purposes.
- ❐ Terms & Conditions accepted.

Apple Books for Authors allows you to self-publish your eBooks and audiobooks directly to their Apple Books storefront.

Account Set-Up Checklist

- ❐ Create login at https://authors.apple.com/.
- ❐ Input banking information for payment.
- ❐ Complete tax information for end-of-year royalty tax purposes.
- ❐ Terms & Conditions accepted.

IngramSpark

IngramSpark allows you to self-publish your eBook, paperback, and hardcover books to the Ingram network of retailers.

IngramSpark can get your book to the following online retailers:

- Amazon.com
- Apple Books
- Barnes&Noble.com
- Barnes & Noble Brick-and-Mortar
- Kobo
- Chapters/Indigo
- Waterstones
- The Book Depository
- Gardners
- Booktopia
- Scribd
- OverDrive
- Bibliotheca
- Hoopla
- Chegg
- EBSCO
- Storytel
- ProQuest
- And many more

Account Set-Up Checklist

- ❐ Create login at https://myaccount.ingramspark.com/Account/Signup.
- ❐ Input banking information for payment.
- ❐ Complete tax information for end-of-year royalty tax purposes. (**NOTE**: Ingram does NOT provide a 1099 for U.S. authors or similar documents for international authors.)
- ❐ Distribution Agreements accepted. IngramSpark distributes to many different retailers. When you sign up with IngramSpark, you will be prompted to sign distribution agreements for a few specific retailers (ex., Apple, Amazon, Target.) **If you plan to go direct with a retailer that**

IngramSpark has distribution with, DO NOT sign that agreement with IngramSpark. You can always sign it later if you decide you don't want the extra login, but once you sign – it is signed! This is where you risk duplicate listings if you sign up everywhere before you have a plan. (If you've already done this, it is fixable – you'll just spend a lot of time with customer service.)

- ❐ Terms & Conditions accepted.

Draft2Digital/Smashwords

Draft2Digital (D2D) acquired Smashwords in 2022. To gain access to both networks to self-publish your eBook and print books, you should sign up with Draft2Digital.

Draft2Digital/Smashwords can get your book to the following online retailers:

- Amazon.com
- Apple Books
- Barnes&Noble.com
- Kobo
- Scribd
- Smashwords
- Tolino

- OverDrive
- Bibliotheca
- Baker & Taylor
- BorrowBox
- Hoopla
- Vivlio

Account Set-Up Checklist

- ❐ Create login at https://www.draft2digital.com/register/.
- ❐ Input banking information for payment.
- ❐ Complete tax information for end-of-year royalty tax purposes.
- ❐ Distribution Agreements accepted.
- ❐ Terms & Conditions accepted.

LuLu allows you to self-publish your eBooks and print books directly to their storefront and network of retailers.

LuLu can get your book to the following online retailers:

- Amazon.com
- Apple Books
- Barnes&Noble.com
- Kobo
- Scribd
- Gardners
- Libri

They also have integrations with Shopify to make it easier for you to sell your book directly from your website.

LuLu also offers additional trim sizes that the other platforms don't provide and additional binding options (e.g., spiral bound). However, some custom sizes and binding types are not always available for distribution to their entire network. Check with LuLu. com to confirm your size and trim will be available to their global distribution network.

Account Set-Up Checklist

- ❒ Create login at https://www.lulu.com/.
- ❒ Input banking information for payment.
- ❒ Complete tax information for end-of-year royalty tax purposes.
- ❒ Terms & Conditions accepted.

Audiobook Creation Exchange (ACX)

Audiobook Creation Exchange (ACX) allows you to self-publish your audiobook to Audible.com, Amazon.com, and Apple. For authors outside the US, UK, Canada, and Ireland, you will not be able to self-publish your audiobook via ACX. Skip to Page 66 for Findaway Voices.

Account Set-Up Checklist

- ❒ Create login at https://www.acx.com/. (You will use your current personal Amazon.com login or you will need to create a new login for your author email address. Amazon is smart though and will know that the two accounts are associated, so you can't leave a review for your own book. Be sure to use the same account that you have for Amazon KDP.)

- ☐ Input banking information for payment.
- ☐ Complete "tax interview" for end-of-year royalty tax purposes.
- ☐ Terms & Conditions accepted.

ACX Exclusivity

Before we go any further, we need to go over a big decision for self-publishing authors who will have an audiobook format for their books.

As with Kindle Select, Amazon understands the value they can pose to subscribers if they can offer "exclusive" content. When Amazon promotes the Audible subscription, they want to highlight to listeners that they are accessing audiobooks that they cannot get anywhere else.

Hence, ACX also offers authors incentives to list their audiobooks exclusively with the platform.

The incentives here are financial (a higher royalty percentage), the ability to set up an audiobook pre-order, and free codes to provide audiobook reviewers.

However, when you are exclusive to ACX, your book will still be available on Audible, Amazon.com, and Apple.

If you plan to hire a narrator through the ACX marketplace and do a royalty share deal, then you must be exclusive to that platform. (That's how ACX will make sure the narrator gets paid.)

You can request to remove a book from exclusivity. If you are in a royalty share deal, you must also have the narrator agree to move the book from exclusivity. They will likely ask for compensation as they will no longer get a royalty split. Consider these factors when making your decision:

Will you hire a narrator through the ACX marketplace with a royalty share deal?
☐ Yes   ☐ No

Will you use (and promote) an audiobook pre-order?
☐ Yes   ☐ No

Will you use (and promote) any free codes for reviewers?
❒ Yes   ❒ No

Based on the research you've done and your vision, will you enroll in ACX Exclusivity and forgo self-publishing your audiobook on other platforms?:

❒ Heck yes, sign me up for ACX exclusivity!
❒ No way, I'm going Wide!
❒ Eh, I'll set it up so I can be exclusive now and if I want to remove it after a year, I'll have the option.

Findaway Voices

Findaway Voices allows you to self-publish your audiobook to many audiobook retailers (including Audible and Amazon).

Findaway Voices can get your book to the following online retailers:

- Amazon.com
- Apple Books
- Nook Audiobooks
- Kobo
- Walmart.com
- Google Play
- Scribd
- OverDrive
- Baker & Taylor
- BAM (Books-A-Million)
- Bibliotheca
- Hoopla
- Libro.FM
- Chirp
- Audiobooks.com
- Storytel
- Radish
- And many more

Account Set-Up Checklist

❒ Create login at https://findawayvoices.com/.
❒ Input banking information for payment.
❒ Complete "tax interview" for end-of-year royalty tax purposes.
❒ Terms & Conditions accepted.

SECTION END:

After working through all the exercises in this section, you should have the following:

- ☐ List of retailers you want your book to appear on.
- ☐ List of platforms that will get you on those retailers.
- ☐ Decision on whether you will enroll your eBook in Kindle Select.
- ☐ Decision on whether you will enroll your audiobook in ACX exclusivity.
- ☐ Platform accounts set-up.

BRICK-AND-MORTAR STRATEGY

Before looking at the pages in this section, go back to the Vision and Goals you listed for your book on Pages 2-6.

Do you envision your book on the shelves at a store or list this as one of your goals?
❑ Yes   ❑ No

If yes, complete this section.

If no, move on to the next section.

I suggest that if you plan to pound the pavement and pursue a brick-and-mortar strategy, you list your print books with IngramSpark. You can set both your wholesale discount and returnability on their system.

When uploading to IngramSpark, ensure you have these settings. (See Pages 240 and 246 for the upload checklist)

❑ Wholesale discount to **55%.**
❑ List your books as **Returnable: Yes – Deliver** or **Returnable: Yes – Destroy**.
❑ Have the price of your book listed on the barcode.

You can change these settings in IngramSpark if you decide to stop this strategy later. The system will show you your expected royalty based on these settings.

You will also need to have a barcode with the retail price listed on the book. We will cover barcodes on Page 169. If this is your strategy, then you must also complete that page of this workbook as well.

I have a video on how I got my book into a local bookstore. It was very exciting. But they carried my book in January 2020... we all know what happened next. I'll revisit a brick-and-mortar strategy again sometime in the future.

Brick-and-mortar stores won't just carry your book without you putting in the effort.

For starters, we need to figure out which stores you will target. Make a list of the bookstores in your area. Include major bookstores (Barnes & Noble or Books-A-Million) and indie bookstores too.

Store	Owner/Manager/ Local Author Contact	Address	Phone Number	Email Address	Social Media Account

Before contacting any of these stores, you must gather some information. Many stores will have some local author programs. However, you aren't the only author in the area. Local stores have been burned by authors who ask for space on the shelves but don't help with sales or foot traffic.

You'll need to create a one-sheet of information on your book, who you are as an author, and your local ties to the community. (Highlight how many people you could bring into their store.)

- ❐ Include on your brick-and-mortar one-sheet:
- ❐ Author Name and Contact Information
- ❐ Book Title and Cover Image
- ❐ Short Book Description
- ❐ ISBN
- ❐ Retail Price
- ❐ Wholesale Discount
- ❐ Short blurbs or reviews (See Page 184)
- ❐ Short bio with any accolades
- ❐ Ties to community (any clubs or groups you belong to? Book clubs are a plus!)
- ❐ Your platform (followers on social media – if you have any)

Before you walk in with your big ask, look at the store's event calendar. Do they do regular readings or book fairs? Have they done book launch events with other authors? Have you attended any of these events?

The same goes for any requests you make of your local library. Do they have a local author program? Can you help them by organizing a reading or workshop? Librarians are tasked with community programming – how can you help?

This script works best for an email or digital message, but be prepared to speak to these points when you are on the phone or talking to the store owner in person:

HELLO,

MY NAME IS _____. I'M A LOCAL AUTHOR, AND MY LATEST BOOK, _____, IS OUT NOW. I HAVE BEEN PROMOTING THE PRE-ORDER, AND I WOULD LOVE TO HAVE THE BOOK AVAILABLE ꜰᴏʀ SALE AT _____.

MY BOOK IS ABOUT
_____
_____.

(YOU CAN FIND IT UNDER ISBN _____)

I CAN OFFER A ___% DISCOUNT TO YOUR STORE, AND I AM WILLING TO DISCUSS A CONSIGNMENT OPTION FOR YOU TO TEST THE DEMAND FOR MY BOOK.

WHAT OTHER DETAILS CAN I PROVIDE YOU WITH?

Instead of ordering a box (or two) of your book from your distributor and handling the inventory and potential returns, some local stores will offer to sell your book on consignment. This means you will put your book on the shelf, and when a customer picks it up and pays for it, the store will get a set percentage. You get the rest. The store takes on no financial liability, and you get paid when a sale is made.

Sounds fair, right?

Well, you are taking on the financial liability. You have to have inventory to bring into the store, let them sit there (unable to sell them elsewhere), and you have already paid the printing and shipping costs.

Before you say yes to a consignment offer, use this worksheet to confirm if you will at least break even. Making the consignment sales at a break-even rate may be worth it. If enough patrons purchase the book, the store may decide to buy a larger box directly from your distributor.

STEP 1: Calculate your cut

Retail Price: $_____

Proposed Consignment Split:

_____% to the bookstore

_____% to the author

_____% to the author X $_____ retail price = **$_____ your cut of the sale.**

STEP 2: Calculate your cost

Price you paid to print the book: $_____

+ Price you paid to ship the book: $_____

+ Any taxes or handling fees for your order: $_____

=ORDER TOTAL: $_____ / #___ of Books in the Order

= $_____ Price per book

STEP 3: Calculate your profit

$_____ your cut of the sale - $_____ price per book = **$_____ your profit.**

(STEP 1)   **(STEP 2)**

Your profit > $0

SECTION END:

After working through all the pages in this section you should have the following:

- ❐ Clarity on your wholesale discount and returnability settings.
- ❐ List of local bookstores to pitch.
- ❐ A completed one-sheet for your book.
- ❐ Confirmation that any potential consignment offers at least break-even.

PRICING AND DISCOUNTS

In this section, we will go over pricing and discounts. While we need to know these strategies before uploading, both are part of your overall marketing strategy. That's right, the price and how you discount the book can make it more (or less) marketable to potential readers and retailers. Remember that the price and the associated royalty are NEVER about how much you want to earn. It is about what your buyer is willing to pay and how much value they think they will derive from your book.

Pricing Strategy

Here is where you will research and record the price you will charge for your book by format. Notice I didn't say that this is where you set the price for your book. Because you don't set the price. Your audience does. Each decision to buy a book or pass on it sets the price for your market.

You will hear about many different pricing strategies among self-publishing authors. Some keep the first book in a series at a very low cost or free to encourage more readers to start the series in the hope they will read the rest of the books. Some will price their books at exactly the average of the other books in their genre.

Your pricing strategy should be set and not easily swayed by shiny objects and a few days of low sales. But it needs to be adaptable to market forces (e.g., inflation).

First, you need to look up the price for books in your genre. Research books that are your closest competitors; similar length, subject matter, etc., and write down their prices below.

eBook Prices   _____   _____   _____   _____

                                 _____   _____   _____   _____

                                 _____   _____   _____   _____

                                 _____   _____   _____   _____

                                 _____   _____   _____   _____

Paperback Prices   _____   _____   _____   _____

                                 _____   _____   _____   _____

                                 _____   _____   _____   _____

                                 _____   _____   _____   _____

                                 _____   _____   _____   _____

                                 _____   _____   _____   _____

Hardcover Prices   _____   _____   _____   _____

                                 _____   _____   _____   _____

                                 _____   _____   _____   _____

                                 _____   _____   _____   _____

                                 _____   _____   _____   _____

                                 _____   _____   _____   _____

Audiobook Prices   _____   _____   _____   _____

                                 _____   _____   _____   _____

                                 _____   _____   _____   _____

                                 _____   _____   _____   _____

                                 _____   _____   _____   _____

                                 _____   _____   _____   _____

Based on these prices, we now need to confirm what you can charge while still earning *something* for your books. All the self-publishing platforms provide a royalty calculator that you can use. **Search "[Platform Name] + Royalty Calculator."** Record the different prices here so you can compare. Change the variables (ex., number of pages, trim size, paper type, binding type, color, etc.) to see how it impacts your royalty. (You'll be able to go back to Page 37 and input these numbers for your Book Profitability exercise.)

I suggest either looking at all the possible prices on one platform and then moving to the next or looking at the potential prices by format. Pick an order that makes sense to you and stick to it. Just make sure you can easily compare the different price points.

Below you will see an example from one of my books. Here I look at all the prices and estimated royalties on one platform before moving to the next. There will be a blank sheet for you to use on the next page:

M.K.'s Example:

Format	Platform	Retail Price	Royalty
eBook	Amazon KDP	$4.99	$3.49
Paperback	Amazon KDP	$12.99	$5.19
Hardcover	Amazon KDP	$19.99	$4.74
Paperback	IngramSpark	$12.99	$5.74
Hardcover	IngramSpark	$19.99	$6.34
eBook	Google Play	$4.99	$3.49
eBook	Draft2Digital/ Smashwords	$4.99	$3.20

Format	Platform	Retail Price	Royalty

Based on these prices, what will you set your book price at?

Format	Price	My Royalty
eBook		
Paperback		
Hardcover		
Audiobook*		

*Reminder you cannot set the price for your audiobook on ACX. Other platforms that allow you to upload audiobooks do offer you the option to set the price.

Next, we will review discounts. There are two main categories of discounts:

1. Promotional Discounts
2. Wholesale/Retailer Discounts

Promotional Discounts

For promotional discounts, let's make a plan. As an author, it is tempting to offer discounts and deals to get people to buy after a slow week of sales. But your price reflects value, so if you are constantly discounting, then perhaps your audience is telling you the book is priced too high. A discount or sale can help give your readers a reason to buy right now, which can be a good thing. But if your audience learns they should just wait for your next discount, you may lose out on sales overall.

Below is a list of the different promotional discounts you may consider. Select the ones you will try. You don't have to pick any; you could pick them all or create new ones not listed below. But remember, you have to promote and market each of these discounts too.

I will allow promotional discounts for...

- ❒ Pre-Orders
- ❒ Holidays/Seasonal Deals
- ❒ Birthdays (My birthday, book birthday, character birthday)
- ❒ Series release
- ❒ Bulk orders (schools or book clubs)

I will offer discounts to...

- ❒ Anyone (setting price lower or distributing discount code to everyone)
- ❒ Email subscribers
- ❒ Social media followers

Wholesale Discounts

Bookstores make money when they sell books. But only if they are buying those books at a discount. Let's say the retail price for your print book is $10. If a bookstore purchases the book from you for $10 (a discount of 0%), and then sells it for $10, they make no money. Actually, they lost money because they had to pay their clerks, cover overhead costs, and manage inventory. Bookstores need to buy your book at a discount so they have some margin on each sale and can make money.

As mentioned on Page 68, the preferred wholesale discount for retailers is 55%. Before we dive into setting this discount, first, you need to answer the following:

Will you self-publish your print book with IngramSpark? (from Page 56)
If no, skip to Page 80.
If yes, run their price calculator to see what you will earn based on your print cost and price.

Will you be opting for a brick-and-mortar strategy (from Page 68).
If no, then set your wholesale discount to the minimum of 30-35% based on the territory.
If yes, set your wholesale discount to 50-55%*.
*Retailers usually like to see a 50-55% wholesale discount.

Format	Price**	Wholesale Discount	My Royalty
Paperback			
Hardcover			

**You can adjust your price and wholesale discount at any time with IngramSpark. They push pricing and discount updates to retailers once a week on Fridays.

I have a video on setting your wholesale discount with IngramSpark that you can reference during this exercise.

SECTION END:

After working through all the checklists in this section you should have the following:

- ❏ Price for your eBook
- ❏ Price for your Paperback
- ❏ Price for your Hardcover
- ❏ Price for your Audiobook
- ❏ Plan for when you will discount

- ❏ Plan for who will be eligible for discounts
- ❏ Plan for how you will communicate discounts

THE SELF-PUBLISHING PROCESS

TECH-SAVVY

how hard is this step?

hard – requires tech skills
& patience!

easy – most every author
can tackle on their own

WRITING

The very first step in self-publishing a book is to write it! While traditional publishing varies by fiction or non-fiction, the book is always step one for self-publishing. You may be using this workbook after your book has been written. In that case, skip to Page 127 for the editing phase.

If you are starting out with just an idea and a desire to write a book, then start in this section. There are worksheets for both fiction (Pages 86-116) and non-fiction (Pages 117-125), as well as exercises and trackers that apply to all genres (Pages 81-85).

Happy writing!

Research

Whether you write fiction or non-fiction (or some amorphous non-narrative hybrid), you must conduct research. Not only will it give your book more shape and credibility, but great writers are also great readers. Let's get to work.

Books in the same genre as my book

Books by authors whose style I want to emulate

Topical Research: Magazines, Podcasts, etc.

Books I want my book listed alongside

Word Count Tracker

Checklists help us see what we need to do and what we have already accomplished. It is doubly beneficial in helping our brains to organize our tasks and gives us some dopamine when we cross something off. Word Count Trackers allow authors to see what we have already done and how much further we have to go.

Some authors live by their daily word count goals. No matter what is going on, they stick to their plan to write that amount. Others like to see how they are doing. Some days they hit their goal, and some days it is a miss, but they can always see that they have made progress.

Maybe you are prolific without needing to track anything. If so, please ignore the word count trackers in this workbook. But, if you like tracking your progress or want to give this a try, then make use of the different trackers on the following pages.

WORD COUNT TRACKER

PLANNED WORD COUNT FOR BOOK:

NUMBER OF DAYS TO REACH GOAL:

WORDS PER DAY GOAL:

DATE	WORDS	TIME	DATE	WORDS	TIME

WORD COUNT TRACKER

PLANNED WORD COUNT FOR BOOK:

NUMBER OF DAYS TO REACH GOAL:

WORDS PER DAY GOAL:

DATE	WORDS	TIME	DATE	WORDS	TIME

WORD COUNT TRACKER

PLANNED WORD COUNT FOR BOOK:

NUMBER OF DAYS TO REACH GOAL:

WORDS PER DAY GOAL:

DATE	WORDS	TIME	DATE	WORDS	TIME

Fiction

If you are writing fiction, the following planning documents are for you. Use them as you need. Most of these exercises are sourced from my book, *How to Write Your First Novel: A Guide For Aspiring Fiction Authors*. Please refer to this book if you need clarity on any of the concepts for planning your first novel.

By no means do you HAVE to do all of these exercises. I find there is a segment of writers who feel they must read every craft book and do every exercise before they can write their book. After procrastinating for years (or decades), they are still writers and not authors – as in no book has materialized. I like to use exercises and craft books when I feel stuck. Once I'm unstuck, I get back to writing my book. I suggest you follow the same pattern, so you don't get into the habit of procrastinating via perfection.

Point of View (POV) and Narrative Structure

What is this story about? (short summary)

_____

_____

_____

_____

_____

_____

_____

_____

_____

_____

_____

_____

_____

_____

Point of view: Who will tell this story?	Narrative Structure: How will you reveal this story?
❏ First-Person ❏ Second-Person ❏ Third-Person ❏ Multiple First-Person Narrators ❏ Third-Person Omniscient	❏ Linear structure ❏ Non-linear structure ❏ Circular structure ❏ Frame narrative ❏ Other

Plot Thickens

This story will be primarily: Plot-driven   Character-driven

What happens in this story? This is different from what the story is about. Here you will write down the events that will occur in the story.

_____

_____

_____

_____

_____

_____

_____

_____

Why this story?

_____

_____

_____

_____

_____

_____

_____

_____

_____

_____

Why this day?

_____

_____

_____

_____

_____

_____

_____

_____

_____

_____

Why this character?

_____

_____

_____

_____

_____

_____

_____

_____

_____

Over the next few pages we will define the main elements of your story.

1. Inciting Incident
2. Rising Action
3. Climax
4. Resolution

But first, what are these main elements? From *How To Write Your First Novel: A Guide for Aspiring Fiction Authors*, here are my definitions:

Inciting Incident

The definition may be self-evident, but this is the event that kicks off your whole story. Some authors may choose to start their story with this incident from the get-go. Bam! Page one. Others may set the scene and introduce at least one or two characters and the setting before this event. Only you can know what is best for your book. But you can't leave the audience hanging for too long. I recommend not going further than the third chapter of your story before introducing this element. Otherwise, the reader may question why they are reading the story. Within the description of this incident, you'll want to explain why your character is involved. Maybe you already set this up in the exposition before this event. If not, you'll need to answer this for the audience.

For example, there was an explosion. Why does your character need to investigate whodunit?

Rising Action

This portion of the book is where your characters get going. The incident has occurred, and now they have to take action. They have to go on a journey. They have to work together. They have to solve the mystery. This is going to be the longest portion of your story. The rising action exposes the clues, the journey twists and turns, and the character is challenged. This is the meat of the story. As the name implies, the stakes should get higher with each new chapter or scene. Throughout this section of your book, you want to be building towards the big reveal or challenge. In subtle ways, you'll need to remind the audience of the stakes involved for your character(s) throughout the story. Remind them why they are on this quest. Why don't they just say, "eh, this is kind of hard. I'll just have a sandwich instead."

Climax

This is it! The moment your story has been building towards. This is the battle royale that your character has been training for. This is when the detective in your novel reveals who committed the crime. This is the moment when your star-crossed lovers can finally be together. To define this moment, ask yourself, what is this story leading towards?

The Climax is usually towards the end of the book in the penultimate chapter. Depending on this moment, you may have several short chapters at the end to bring the energy up as this final moment draws closer. If you know what this moment will be from the beginning, you can pepper in the right amount of foreshadowing and clues along the way. If not, you'll need to go back through the manuscript to add these elements in.

Resolution

The Resolution should be a relatively short section to close out the story. Now that the problem has been solved, the criminal brought to justice, and the world set right, it is time to wrap up any loose ends. This is where you can give your characters their happily ever after. Or, you can plant the seeds for a sequel. It is typically the final chapter of your book.

Inciting Incident Rising Action Climax Resolution

What is the Inciting Incident?

_____

_____

_____

_____

_____

_____

_____

_____

_____

_____

_____

_____

_____

_____

_____

_____

_____

_____

_____

_____

_____

Inciting Incident   **Rising Action**   Climax   Resolution

What are the elements of your Rising Action?

_____

_____

_____

_____

_____

_____

_____

_____

_____

_____

_____

_____

_____

_____

_____

_____

_____

_____

_____

_____

_____

_____

Inciting Incident   Rising Action   **Climax**   Resolution

How will the story reach a Climax? What will happen here?

_____

_____

_____

_____

_____

_____

_____

_____

_____

_____

_____

_____

_____

_____

_____

_____

_____

_____

_____

_____

_____

_____

Inciting Incident   Rising Action   Climax   **Resolution**

How will you Resolve the story? Will you leave a cliff hanger for a subsequent novel?

_____

_____

_____

_____

_____

_____

_____

_____

_____

_____

_____

_____

_____

_____

_____

_____

_____

_____

_____

_____

_____

_____

_____

_____

Primary Plots and Subplots

First, let's detail your primary plot:

_____

_____

_____

_____

_____

But that won't be the only thing happening in your story. Remember that you do not have to have exactly four subplots just because I give you room for that on this sheet. That may be too much to manage. Use this space to provide a brief sentence or two about the other plots going on that will impact your characters:

Subplot 1:	Subplot 2:

Subplot 3:	Subplot 4:

Character Description Sheets

Keep track of the details and biographical information about your characters. You can use all of these details, some of them, or even add more as needed. I've provided six sheets in this workbook. Add more as you need them.

Character Name:

(PUT IMAGE OF AVATAR OR DREAM CASTING FOR CHARACTER HERE)

Date of birth:

Race:

Gender:

Orientation:

Hair Color:

Eye Color:

Height:

Weight/Body Type:

Hometown:

Relationships with other characters:

Character Name:

FEARS	MOTIVATIONS

INSECURITIES	SUPER SKILLS

Character Name:

(PUT IMAGE OF AVATAR
OR DREAM CASTING
FOR CHARACTER HERE)

Date of birth:

Race:

Gender:

Orientation:

Hair Color:

Eye Color:

Height:

Weight/Body Type:

Hometown:

Relationships with other characters:

Character Name:

FEARS	MOTIVATIONS

INSECURITIES	SUPER SKILLS

Character Name:

(PUT IMAGE OF AVATAR
OR DREAM CASTING
FOR CHARACTER HERE)

Date of birth:

Race:

Gender:

Orientation:

Hair Color:

Eye Color:

Height:

Weight/Body Type:

Hometown:

Relationships with other characters:

Character Name:

FEARS

MOTIVATIONS

INSECURITIES

SUPER SKILLS

Character Name:

(PUT IMAGE OF AVATAR
OR DREAM CASTING
FOR CHARACTER HERE)

Date of birth:

Race:

Gender:

Orientation:

Hair Color:

Eye Color:

Height:

Weight/Body Type:

Hometown:

Relationships with other characters:

Character Name:

FEARS	MOTIVATIONS

INSECURITIES	SUPER SKILLS

Character Name:

(PUT IMAGE OF AVATAR
OR DREAM CASTING
FOR CHARACTER HERE)

Date of birth:

Race:

Gender:

Orientation:

Hair Color:

Eye Color:

Height:

Weight/Body Type:

Hometown:

Relationships with other characters:

Character Name:

FEARS	MOTIVATIONS

INSECURITIES	SUPER SKILLS

Character Name:

(PUT IMAGE OF AVATAR
OR DREAM CASTING
FOR CHARACTER HERE)

Date of birth:

Race:

Gender:

Orientation:

Hair Color:

Eye Color:

Height:

Weight/Body Type:

Hometown:

Relationships with other characters:

Character Name:

FEARS	MOTIVATIONS

INSECURITIES	SUPER SKILLS

Realistic Characters Activities

You can do many exercises to help build a backstory for your characters. The characters don't exist in a vacuum; they should read as though they are fully formed people (or creatures). These are some of the exercises I do when I am feeling stuck or notice that my main or side characters are feeling a little flat.

Write a letter from the character's point of view. Start with the line: "If you're reading this, then..."

_____

_____

_____

_____

_____

_____

_____

_____

_____

_____

_____

_____

_____

_____

_____

_____

_____

_____

Where does your character fit into their family? This is an exercise where you can go into some detail about their parents, siblings, cousins, etc. Or maybe this character never knew their family and had to make one of their own.

_____

_____

_____

_____

_____

_____

_____

_____

_____

_____

_____

_____

_____

_____

_____

_____

_____

_____

_____

_____

_____

_____

_____

Start a journal entry from your character's point of view. "I think I can pinpoint my _____ back to this one event in my childhood. Here is how it all started..."

_____

_____

_____

_____

_____

_____

_____

_____

_____

_____

_____

_____

_____

_____

_____

_____

_____

_____

_____

_____

_____

_____

What is the character's astrological sign? (I sometimes switch this out for their Enneagram number.) How do they embody or defy this trait?

_____

_____

_____

_____

_____

_____

_____

_____

_____

_____

_____

_____

_____

_____

_____

_____

_____

_____

_____

_____

_____

_____

Believable Villains Exercises

These exercises will focus on retelling your story from your villain's point of view. Remember, they think they are the hero in their own story.

How did your villain and hero first meet/interact?

_____

_____

_____

_____

_____

_____

_____

_____

_____

_____

_____

_____

_____

_____

_____

_____

_____

_____

_____

What is the Inciting Incident for your book? How did your villain experience this event?

_____

_____

_____

_____

_____

_____

_____

_____

_____

_____

_____

_____

_____

_____

_____

_____

_____

_____

_____

_____

_____

What is the Resolution to your story? How did your villain experience this event?

_____

_____

_____

_____

_____

_____

_____

_____

_____

_____

_____

_____

_____

_____

_____

_____

_____

_____

_____

_____

_____

Why does this character think they are a hero?

Non-Fiction

If you are writing a work of non-fiction, the following planning documents are for you. Use them as you need.

By no means do you HAVE to do all of these exercises. I find there is a segment of writers who feel they must read every craft book and do every exercise before they can write their book. After procrastinating for years (or decades), they are still writers and not authors – as in no book has materialized. I like to use exercises and craft books when I feel stuck. Once I'm unstuck, I get back to writing my book. I suggest you follow the same pattern, so you don't get into the habit of procrastinating via perfection.

What's your point? – Thesis

Just like your high school term paper, you need a thesis. Let's walk through these exercises to help you narrow this down:

What will someone learn when they read your book? When your reader puts it down after the last page, what will they know that they didn't before reading?

_____

_____

_____

_____

_____

_____

(Or perhaps this will help you define it better) What will they be able and empowered to do?

_____

_____

_____

_____

_____

_____

_____

_____

Who is this book for? (It CANNOT be everyone!)

_____

_____

_____

_____

_____

_____

_____

_____

_____

_____

Now that we have a clearer idea of your thesis write that here. It should be no longer than one paragraph. It can be as short as two sentences, depending on how concise you can be.

_____

_____

_____

_____

_____

_____

_____

_____

_____

How is your book different from other books on the topic?

Writing a book is a big commitment and a lot of work. As much as you love the idea for your book now, when you are in the thick of writing, you need to remember how your book is different and distinct from others in your genre. Because if it isn't, this thought will pop up and derail you: "Maybe the audience should just read X book instead, and I can get my time back." I've seen it happen. You need to know how your book is distinct and why it needs to be out there.

How is this book different from others on the same topic?

_____

_____

_____

_____

_____

What perspective do you have that other authors don't have? What makes you unique in writing this book?

_____

_____

_____

_____

Or if it is the first and one-of-a-kind, then why are you the one to finally write it? Why has no one else written this book?

_____

_____

_____

_____

_____

How do you know this?

If you put this information into your book, you must show *how* you know it. You must cite those sources in your bibliography if you are using data, arguments, or information that others worked to put together. If you need to gather information, make a list to ensure you find that data. Keep in mind that the credibility of your sources will be the foundation for your argument. If you build it on shaky information, it can completely fall apart under scrutiny.

What you know from:

Life experience:

_____

_____

_____

_____

_____

_____

Information and opinions put forth by experts in your field:

(**NOTE**: Be sure to find experts from diverse backgrounds. Not just in terms of race, gender, or orientation. But find experts who disagree with you, those who have more experience than you, and some starting out. Don't just find clones of yourself.)

_____

_____

_____

_____

_____

_____

_____

Case studies:

_____

_____

_____

_____

_____

_____

Data from credible sources (what are the top impartial data sources for your field?):

_____

_____

_____

_____

_____

_____

Interviews (list your ideal interviewees and what you aim to learn from this conversation):

_____

_____

_____

_____

_____

How will you show your reader and bring them along with you? How will you most effectively construct your book for the reader to follow and comprehend it?

Looking back at your thesis, let's map out HOW you will show your reader this information. How will you create a foundation in the early chapters so you can add more advanced topics and arguments later in the book?

You may not break your book into parts and sections when you write it, but this can help you outline how you will build your argument. You do not need to use each space provided. Maybe you only see three major sections of your book. Perhaps you envision more sections with fewer chapters in each. Use what you need, and leave what you don't.

Book Sections

1. _____

   a. What will the reader KNOW by the end of this section?

   _____

   _____

   _____

2. _____

   a. What will the reader KNOW by the end of this section?

   _____

   _____

   _____

3. _____

   a. What will the reader KNOW by the end of this section?

   _____

   _____

   _____

4. _____

    a. What will the reader KNOW by the end of this section?

    _____

    _____

    _____

5. _____

    a. What will the reader KNOW by the end of this section?

    _____

    _____

    _____

Chapters in Section 1

1. _____
2. _____
3. _____
4. _____
5. _____

Chapters in Section 2

1. _____
2. _____
3. _____
4. _____
5. _____

Chapters in Section 3

1. _____
2. _____
3. _____
4. _____
5. _____

Chapters in Section 4

1. _____
2. _____
3. _____
4. _____
5. _____

Chapters in Section 5

1. _____
2. _____
3. _____
4. _____
5. _____

Does it need to be a graph/image?

I include this here because I see two types of non-fiction authors. The first type wants to use charts, graphs, and images to explain everything. They are visual learners and teachers. The other type meticulously writes out everything instead of using a visual aid. The best option is a balance somewhere between the extremes. Images and graphs in your book will add to the design and print cost. But they should not be avoided entirely, either. You may find your book doesn't need any visuals, and that is okay.

Let's evaluate:

Am I having trouble explaining this with words? (ex. exponential growth or compounding interest)

☐ Yes   ☐ No

If you could only post images on your social media platform and wanted to communicate this point, how might you represent this concept visually?

_____

_____

_____

Can the words stand on their own without a graph or chart?

☐ Yes   ☐ No

Will this visual help readers who benefit from visual learning, or is this a personal preference?

☐ Yes   ☐ No

Does the image enhance my argument?

☐ Yes   ☐ No

Can the image be portrayed in Black and White?

☐ Yes   ☐ No

Celebration planning

You just finished your book. So many writers never make it here. In a sea of unfinished manuscripts, yours is done. The words are together and clean. This is a huge moment. While there is still more to do, this is a significant accomplishment worth celebrating! You did it! You. Wrote. A. Book!

How will I celebrate this milestone?

_____

_____

_____

_____

_____

_____

Who will I celebrate with?

_____

_____

_____

_____

_____

_____

Special food/drinks:

_____

_____

_____

_____

_____

EDITING

When creating a book, editing is just as important as writing. There is no way you get it perfect on the first go. Or the second. Or the third. Editing takes time. It means stepping away from your manuscript before coming back to it. It means letting someone else look at it and give you their critical opinion. Below is the master checklist of all the steps for editing that I recommend. I will break down each step in this section.

After writing your book, this will be the most time-intensive process. And it should be. You should go through the manuscript several times, and you'll need to give your readers and editors time as well. Whenever your manuscript is out of your hands and with a reader or editor, here are two things to remember:

1. DON'T YOU DARE MAKE ANY CHANGES TO THE MANUSCRIPT! This can create two different versions of the book, and then you have to marry the edits with the new version. Hold your new ideas until you have all your edits back and incorporate them all at once.
2. You can still get work done on the book even if you can't touch the manuscript. Use these times to research your self-publishing strategy and get your technical setup in place.

Editing Process Master Checklist:

- ❐ Draft 1 completed
- ❐ First Self-Edit
- ❐ Draft 2 – make changes based on initial self-edit
- ❐ Send to First Reader
- ❐ Draft 3 – Incorporate Edits from First Reader
- ❐ Alpha Reader Review
- ❐ Incorporate Alpha Reader Edits
- ❐ Developmental Edits
- ❐ Incorporate Developmental Edits
- ❐ Beta Readers
- ❐ Incorporate Beta Reader Edits
- ❐ Copy Edit 1
- ❐ Incorporate Edits
- ❐ Copy Edit 2
- ❐ Incorporate Edits
- ❐ Final Proofread (after formatting)

Self-Edits/Revisions Checklist

Your first editor is: you! You can be your worst critic sometimes, or perhaps you are the devil on your own shoulder saying that the long rambling monologue can absolutely stay. Either way, you know your weaknesses. And you know when you decided to change characters' names mid-manuscript. Your self-edits will start the process of turning your manuscript into a polished book. Here are the elements I always look at each time I work through self-edits.

⧗ When To Tackle

One to two weeks after you finish the first draft. Give the manuscript a little bit of time to breathe and your brain a chance to relax.

Self-Edits:

- ❏ Save your manuscript as a new file + "Draft 2".
- ❏ Enable track changes so you can see what you have changed or modified.
- ❏ Keep track of the following questions:

What could be more clear?	What was left unresolved?
What was repeated?	What was missed entirely?

Highlight character names and any dates/locations mentioned. As you go through each round of edits, you will better catch where there are any discrepancies. You know where you need to do more work.

Details to Track:

_____

_____

_____

_____

_____

_____

_____

_____

_____

_____

_____

_____

_____

_____

_____

_____

_____

You may need to do two or three rounds of self-edits before you move to the next phase.

First Reader and Alpha Readers

Not every author works with First Readers or Alpha Readers. My **First Reader** is always my husband. He keeps me motivated and sees the worst of every draft. Then by the time it goes to the next person, it is passable.

Alpha Readers (and Beta Readers) should read in your genre. They should like the type of book you have written and often read books like it. That way, you know any critiques are on the story, not trying to turn your western romance into science fiction. I would define an Alpha Reader as someone who reads an early draft or even pages, whereas Beta Readers see a more developed manuscript. Ideally, the book is more polished by the time you get to Beta Readers, but they can still give you good feedback for improvement.

Who is your Alpha Reader going to be? (I recommend one or two)

_____

_____

 Before you send your manuscript to anyone, ensure it is in ONE document. DO NOT send them a collection of individual documents for each chapter.

ONE DOCUMENT

When you send your book off to your Alpha Reader, here are the details you need to include:

Feedback Due Date: _____

Feedback You Are Looking For: (Usually, at this point, you are looking for plot and big-picture feedback. If they also find typos, cool.)

_____

_____

_____

_____

_____

_____

_____

_____

_____

_____

_____

Notes from your Alpha Reader(s). What are the major themes and comments from their review?

_____

_____

_____

_____

_____

_____

_____

_____

_____

_____

_____

_____

_____

_____

Incorporate Edits/Full Read-Through and Self-Edits

Now that you have the initial feedback, it is time to make your revisions as a new draft.

Draft Start Date:
Estimated Draft Completion Date:

- ❏ Save your manuscript as a new file + "Draft 3".
- ❏ Enable track changes so you can see what you have changed or modified.
- ❏ Keep track of the following items:

Focus for this round of edits

Highlight character names and any dates/locations mentioned. As you go through your second round of edits, you will better catch where there are any discrepancies. You know where you need to do more work.

Details to Track:

_____

_____

_____

_____

_____

_____

_____

_____

_____

_____

_____

_____

_____

_____

_____

_____

_____

_____

_____

Story/Developmental Editing

You may feel that your Alpha Reader nailed it at this point, and they found every potential story issue with your book. Maybe you are part of a Critique Group or have a seasoned Critique Partner who has resolved the lingering issues. If so, great! Move on to the next round of revisions on Page 139.

But perhaps you don't have someone who can be an Alpha Reader or Critique Partner for you, and you need to hire someone to do a developmental review. I've worked with editors who define developmental editing as reading through and identifying holes or structural issues and making suggestions to fix them. I've worked with others who see developmental editing as co-writing a book with the author. The pricing varies accordingly.

Before you research developmental editors, you should figure out what you need. Do you want someone to verify that the story or thesis is secure? Do you want someone to co-write with you? Once you know what help you need, you can start to research editors. If you feel confident in your Alpha Reader's or Critique Partner's skillset, you can forgo hiring a developmental editor altogether.

Where to find a great editor: You should use one or all of these options to find different editors to work with. Keep in mind that the longer your list, the harder it will be to whittle it down. First, we need a list to work from:

- ❏ Search for Developmental or Story Editors on Reedsy. Check the reviews and only add Developmental Editors to your list whose style you like.

- ❏ Search for Developmental or Story Editors on YouTube. You can get a feel for their style and how they communicate/teach with their comments.

- ❏ Ask for recommendations in writing groups on social media.

- ❏ Ask other indie authors for recommendations.

- ❏ On the following pages you will find a chart to compare your editing options.

VETTING POTENTIAL EDITORS

It is essential to ask the editors questions at this stage. You will be able to whittle down your list quickly as you find out who is in and out of your price range, who has the experience to help, and who communicates with you. A few critical items to ask:

- What is your pricing model? Flat rate, word count, or hourly? Do you require full prepaymen t, or will you take a down payment?

- What is included in the price? How many rounds of revision will be included? Will you provide an editorial letter?

- What is your availability, and how quickly do you turn your review around?

- What genre do you usually edit? Do you have experience with self-published books or traditionally published books?

- How do you communicate? (What questions are they asking you? Do you think you will mesh well?)

Comparing Developmental Editors

Editor	Contact Info	Quoted Price	Full payment up front or down payment accepted?	Experience with books in my genre?	Review rounds included?	Estimated start and end date?

Editor	Contact Info	Quoted Price	Full payment up front or down payment accepted?	Experience with books in my genre?	Review rounds included?	Estimated start and end date?

Editor	Contact Info	Quoted Price	Full payment up front or down payment accepted?	Experience with books in my genre?	Review rounds included?	Estimated start and end date?

Incorporate Edits/Full Read-Through and Self-Edits

Now that you have the developmental feedback, it is time to make your revisions as a new draft. Once completed, send back the draft to the editor if you have more than one round in your agreement.

Draft Start Date:
Estimated Draft Completion Date:

- ❏ Save your manuscript as a new file + "Draft 4".
- ❏ Enable track changes so you can see what you have changed or modified.
- ❏ Keep track of the following items:

Focus for this round of edits

Highlight areas your editor called out, and any text moved. As you go through your next round of edits, you will better catch where there are any discrepancies. You know where you need to do more work.

Details to Track:

_____

_____

_____

_____

_____

_____

_____

_____

_____

_____

_____

_____

_____

_____

_____

_____

_____

_____

_____

_____

Beta Readers

Next up are your Beta Readers. If you used a Developmental Editor, you might feel your book is solid and that you do not need to work with Beta Readers (and vice versa). However, a potential route if you think that Developmental Editing is out of your budget may be able to crowdsource story and structural feedback from a small group of dedicated Beta Readers.

Beta Readers are those who have agreed to read your manuscript and provide critical feedback on what is not clear, what could be improved, and how. If you are part of a critique group, they may become your de facto Beta Readers. You may have assembled a trusted group of fellow authors to be your Beta Readers. The important things to note are that they:

1. Read and enjoy your genre.
2. Will commit to reading the book by a given date.
3. Can give critical feedback on content, not just typos and grammar.

> ▶️ I have a video on how to make the most of working with your Beta Readers. Watch this before you start signing up readers for your team.

Do you have people in mind who fit these criteria? Ideally, I like to have four or five Beta Readers. Too many, and you spend all your time herding cats and dealing with potentially conflicting information.

My Beta Readers:

_____

_____

_____

_____

_____

_____

_____

_____

Confirm with each person that they are available and committed to helping you out BEFORE you send the manuscript.

PRO TIP Add a watermark to your manuscript with the Beta Reader's name on it. It is a nice touch for that reader. Also, if you are nervous about any of your book being leaked, then you can see who did it.

When you send your book off to your Beta Readers, here are the details you need to include:

Feedback Due Date: _____

Feedback You Are Looking For: (Usually at this point you are looking for plot and big picture feedback. If they also find typos, cool.)

_____

_____

_____

_____

_____

_____

_____

_____

_____

_____

_____

_____

_____

_____

Notes from your Beta Reader(s): What are the major themes and comments from their review? DO NOT START MAKING ANY EDITS UNTIL ALL FEEDBACK IS IN. You are looking for consensus on what is unclear and what needs fixing. Not a mutant manuscript that is trying to make everyone happy. Synthesize their comments and proceed accordingly.

Incorporate Edits/Full Read-Through and Self-Edits

Now that you have all the Beta Reader feedback, it is time to make your revisions as a new draft. Again, do not start to make edits until everyone has sent their comments back and you can synthesize the notes. Often there will be conflicting suggestions. You need to sort through that first before changing your manuscript. You are the author and have the ultimate say.

Draft Start Date:
Estimated Draft Completion Date:

- ❏ Save your manuscript as a new file + "Draft 5".
- ❏ Enable track changes so you can see what you have changed or modified.
- ❏ Keep track of the following items:

Focus for this round of edits

Highlight any areas where there is conflicting feedback. Something needs to be changed, but you need to figure out what that will be. As you go through your next round of edits, you will better catch where there are any discrepancies. You know where you need to do more work.

Details to Track:

_____

_____

_____

_____

_____

_____

_____

_____

_____

_____

_____

_____

_____

_____

_____

_____

_____

_____

_____

_____

Copy Editing

Before you do any copy editing, you should feel 100% set on the meat of your book. We are done building and refining the structure. The plot and content are set. When we start copy edits, we tweak and correct typos and grammar. Do not start copy editing if you have any hesitations about your plot, character, or significant book elements. Especially if you end up paying for a copy editor. If you have the book edited for grammar and typos and then go back and add whole new sections, you must start again with another round of copy editing.

You may feel that your Beta Readers were thorough in both content and typos. I assure you; they were not. Each person so far who has looked at your manuscript is human. They miss things. Even the best, most dedicated copy editor may catch 90% of your errors. That leaves 10%. We want to be very thorough at this point.

Thankfully, copy editing services are less expensive than developmental editing. It is the more affordable of the two and will bring out the best in your book. And even with a copy editor, you can expect a typo or "too" to be left behind; even some of the most well-known books have them.

Where to find a great editor: You should use one or all of these options to find different editors to work with. Keep in mind that the longer your list, the harder it will be to whittle it down. Right now, we are looking at making a list of potential editors. We will whittle down next.

- ☐ Search for Copy Editors on Reedsy. Check the reviews and only add editors to your list whose communication style you like.

- ☐ Search for Copy Editors on Fiverr. Check the reviews and only add editors to your list whose communication style you like.

- ☐ Search for Copy Editors on YouTube. You can get a feel for their style and how they communicate/teach with their comments.

- ☐ Ask for recommendations in writing groups on social media.

- ☐ Ask other indie authors for recommendations.

- ☐ On the following pages you will find a chart to compare your editing options.

VETTING POTENTIAL EDITORS

It is essential to ask questions at this stage. You will be able to whittle down your list quickly as you find out who is in and out of your price range, who has the experience to help, and who communicates with you. A few critical questions to ask:

- What is your pricing model? Is the rate per hour or per word? Do you require prepayment, or will you take a down payment?

- What is included in the price? How many rounds of revision will be included?

- What is your availability, and how quickly do you turn around your review?

- What genre do you usually edit? Do you have experience with self-published books or traditionally published books?

- How do you communicate? (What questions are they asking you? Do you think you will mesh well?)

Comparing Copy Editors

Editor	Contact Info	Quoted Price	Full payment up front or down payment accepted?	Experience with books in my genre?	Review rounds included?	Estimated start and end date?

Editor	Contact Info	Quoted Price	Full payment up front or down payment accepted?	Experience with books in my genre?	Review rounds included?	Estimated start and end date?

Editor	Contact Info	Quoted Price	Full payment up front or down payment accepted?	Experience with books in my genre?	Review rounds included?	Estimated start and end date?

Incorporate Edits/Full Read-Through and Self-Edits

Now that you have feedback from your copy editor, it is time to make your revisions as a new draft. At the end, you may feel the book is done. Some authors I have worked with do a second copy edit after they finish incorporating the edits from the first copy edit. If you feel it needs another review, you'll do that AFTER incorporating this round. That way, the manuscript is cleaner, and the final errors will be easier to pick through. If you do a second copy edit, you'll have a Draft 7 and will incorporate those edits before moving on to Page 153.

Draft Start Date:
Estimated Draft Completion Date:

- ❑ Save your manuscript as a new file + "Draft 6".
- ❑ Enable track changes so you can see what you have changed or modified.
- ❑ Keep track of the following items:

Focus for this round of edits

There should not be any plot elements to track. Still, you will want to pay close attention to what words you consistently capitalize, what grammar rules you are using, if you are consistent in how they are applied, and any other minor typos you often make. We are fine-tuning at this point.

Details to Track:

_____

_____

_____

_____

_____

_____

_____

_____

_____

_____

_____

_____

_____

_____

_____

_____

_____

_____

_____

_____

Final Self-Edit and Read-Through

At this point, your book should be as perfect as it will be. But you are not done editing yet. (Ultimately, you should finish the editing phase feeling so utterly sick of your book. Then you know you've done enough.) Before you send the book to formatting, you should have done at least one edit where you read the text out loud. I recommend that this is the final edit.

When you are reading your book aloud, you will catch more fine-tuning edits. While the copy may be technically accurate, when you read it aloud, you will notice repetitive word use or alliteration that wasn't intended.

When I do this, I record my audiobook. I narrate my books, so this gives me a chance to do the final read-through and record my audio all at once. If you don't intend to self-narrate your audiobook (or even do an audiobook), you may want to use auto-narration in Microsoft Word so you can hear the words without ruining your voice.

Read Aloud Edit

- ❏ Read aloud and record.
- ❏ Use auto-narration to hear your text.

If you plan to have an audiobook format for your book, we will focus on that process next. Especially if you are planning to self-narrate, this is the phase in your process when we will do this work. If you plan to have a professional narrate, you may start that process concurrent with your print and eBook formatting. If you are not sure you want to have an audiobook format or you feel that this will be something you want to add later, you can skip ahead to Page 158 and come back to this section later.

Self-Narrating Your Audiobook

If you have elected to self-narrate your audiobook, you will need to pack a lot of patience. You should enjoy acting and elect to do this because you think you can bring the best voice to the book, not just to save money. Here are the steps to self-narrate your book.

Self-Narrating Checklist

- ❏ Save the final manuscript as a separate, new file, "[TITLE] Audiobook Script."
- ❏ Read through and remove any words or phrases that are for print only. (Ex. "As you can see in this chart below...")
- ❏ Purchase a good microphone. Do not use the built-in microphone on your computer or your cell phone. I use the ATR2100 microphone. In the past, I have also used the Blue Snowball and Blue Yeti microphones.
- ❏ Download Audacity or use professional recording and editing software. (Audacity is free!) Wondershare Filmora is another option.
- ❏ Watch tutorials on the recording and editing software that you selected.
- ❏ Start recording:
  - ○ Save each chapter as a separate file.
  - ○ You may want to go back through and re-record your first chapters when you finish recording the whole book.
  - ○ Record any bonus content you wish to offer at this time as well.
- ❏ Edit your files to match the platform requirements.
- ❏ Run your files through ACX Audio Lab. https://www.acx.com/audiolab. Even if you don't plan to publish with ACX, this system can help you catch any issues.

▶ I have several videos on how I have narrated my own audiobooks and my tips. Check out my number one tip for narrating your audiobook to get you started.

RECORDING TIPS:

- Stay hydrated.

- Record for 30 minutes at a time to ensure you don't get into too much of a flow. You may get monotone and talk too fast.

- Decide if you will record in chronological order or record the shortest chapters first. Either method could work. It's a personal choice.

OPENING AND CLOSING CREDITS

Each platform requires you to have Opening Credits, Closing Credits, and a Retail Sample. The Retail Sample can be the first five minutes or just the best five minutes. Your Opening and Closing Credits need to follow a specific script. You can add a bit, but these elements are the bare minimum:

<u>Opening Credits</u>	<u>Closing Credits</u>
"[title of audiobook]"	The End
"[subtitle if applicable]"	
Written & Narrated by [name of author]	Thank you for listening to
Copyright YYYY	[title of audiobook]

Before you begin, let's examine the three phases of self-narrating your audiobook. When a professional audiobook publishing house produces an audiobook, they go through all of these phases (and a casting step as well), and they have sound engineers to help them execute each one. Don't be intimidated. You can do this too. You can produce your audiobook by working through these three phases: Recording, Editing, and Mastering:

Record (Audiobook) – When you elect to narrate your own audiobook, the recording phase is when you sit down (in a quiet place with no ambient noise), hit record, and start narrating the book. This phase can tax your voice, so stay hydrated and take breaks often. This will rest your voice and help you keep your energy up while narrating.

Edit (Audiobook) – This is the phase when recorded audiobook files are cleaned up. Coughs. Rustling paper. The ten times you flubbed the same line over and over. All those little mess-ups are removed in this phase. You complete editing when you have one MP4 file for each chapter of your book.

Master (Audiobook) – This is the phase when your edited MP4 files are polished. If you recorded this chapter in two settings, you will balance the volume and ensure the decibels don't peak too high. You don't want your listeners to jump if it gets too loud too quickly. In this phase, you will ensure each file meets the requirements for uploading and submitting.

Use the tracking sheet on the next page to stay organized as you create your self-narrated audiobook.

Audiobook Recording Tracker

Chapter/ Section Title	Recorded	Edited	Mastered	Audio Lab Check	Uploaded

Hiring a Professional to Narrate Your Audiobook

Suppose you don't feel particularly excited about self-narrating or don't want to spend your precious energy and effort learning how to record and edit. In that case, you may elect to hire a voice actor (or multiple) to narrate your book. I also include using A.I. technology in this. You are hiring a narrator; they just aren't human. Use the same questions and scrutiny regarding price, sound quality, etc. when deciding between a human or A.I. narrator.

Where to find a great voice actor: You should use one or all of these options to find different narrators to work with. Keep in mind that the longer your list, the harder it will be to whittle it down. Right now, we are looking at making a list of potential narrators. We will whittle down next.

- ❐ Search for voice actors on ACX Marketplace.
- ❐ Search for voice actors on Findaway Voices Marketplace.
- ❐ Search for A.I. powered narration tools and confirm which are approved to upload to your selected platforms.
- ❐ Ask for recommendations in writing groups on social media.
- ❐ Ask other indie authors for recommendations.

Refer back to Page 66, where you outlined your plan for whether you will be exclusive to ACX or not. Your decision will impact whether you use a platform-specific marketplace to find and pay your narrator.

VETTING POTENTIAL NARRATORS

It is essential to ask questions at this stage. You will be able to whittle down your list quickly as you find out who is in and out of your price range, who has the experience to help, and who communicates with you. A few critical items to consider:

- What is your experience narrating books?

- What is your pricing model? Are you open to a royalty split, or do you want to be paid upfront?

- What is included in the price? Are you willing to narrate additional bonus content? Are you willing to do some marketing around the audiobook with me?

- Will you provide the finished files ready to submit to the platform, or will I have to have those mastered by someone else?

- What is your availability, and how quickly do you turn around your narration?

- How do you communicate? (What questions are they asking you? Do you think you will mesh well?)

Celebration planning

You have a final book in your hands. It has been revised and edited and is now ready to go out into the world, almost. The book is done, and with all of this momentum, nothing can stop you now. Pause and celebrate this big step!

How will I celebrate this milestone?

_____

_____

_____

_____

_____

Who will I celebrate with?

_____

_____

_____

_____

_____

Special food/drinks:

_____

_____

_____

_____

TECHNICAL SET UP – ISBNS, COPYRIGHT, AND BARCODES, OH MY!

Now for the fun part, where you take off your writer and creative hat and put on your publisher hat. Getting your book set up to publish takes time, patience, and attention to detail.

In this section, we'll go over how to register your book with the appropriate agencies so that it has its best possible chance to meet your vision.

TECH-SAVVY

how hard is this step?

hard – requires tech skills & patience!

easy – most every author can tackle on their own

The technical savvy required for this section is minimal. All of these elements include going to a website, setting up an account, and filling out a simple form. Yes, some of these steps involve registering with a government entity. That can be intimidating, but it is very straightforward if you have done the work up to this point.

I see many authors get tripped up on this step for two reasons:

1. They rushed and completed this step before they had their strategy in place.
2. They told themselves this was a complex and highly technical step that only technology mavens could handle.

DISCLAIMER TIME

We will also review your options regarding copyright and business registrations. I AM NOT A LAWYER. I AM NOT AN ACCOUNTANT. I am certainly not your lawyer or accountant. In this section, I will give you a starting point for researching decisions with legal and tax implications. It is on you to finish that research and consult with the appropriate professionals based on the laws in your state/country as well as your individual tax situation.

> I have several videos on ISBNs, Barcodes, Library of Congress Numbers, and the like. Check out my video, where I break down the difference between these important elements.

Here's an overview of what each format will require.

Each format requires its own ISBN. Only physical books require barcodes. And the entire work is eligible for a Library of Congress Number and a Copyright Registration:

YOUR BOOK

eBook	Paperback	Hardcover	Audiobook
	1 Barcode	1 Barcode	
1 ISBN	1 ISBN	1 ISBN	1 ISBN
1 Library of Congress Number			
1 Copyright Registration			

ISBNs

ISBNs or **International Standard Book Numbers** are the social security number for your book.

It is the unique number used to identify that exact book down to the format and edition.

You need one ISBN for each format of your book. The ISBN for that format is the same across any retailers or platforms. If you plan to publish your eBook wide on multiple platforms, you will have one ISBN you use wherever you upload the eBook. (This is why "free" ISBNs from the platforms are an issue. You can usually only use them with that platform.)

> Your ISBNs will be listed on the interior copyright page (Page 167) and must be input into each self-publishing platform when you upload.

EXAMPLE 1

Author 1	ISBNs Needed
eBook	1
Paperback	1
TOTAL:	**2 ISBNs**

EXAMPLE 2

Author 2	ISBNs Needed
eBook	1
Paperback	1
Hardcover	1
Audiobook	1
TOTAL:	**4 ISBNs**

How many ISBNs do you need?

Add a "1" next to each of your selected formats	ISBNs Needed
eBook	
Paperback	
Hardcover	
Audiobook	
Large Print	
TOTAL:	

WHERE DO YOU GET YOUR ISBN?

Most countries have one official agency that provides ISBNs to authors and publishers. This could be a department of the government or a private agency.

ISBNs are usually non-transferrable and should only be purchased or acquired from the official agency. Make sure you get your ISBNs from the correct agency.

Official ISBN source for some of the largest self-publishing countries:

U.S.: Bowker
https://www.myidentifiers.com/

U.K.: Nielsen
https://www.nielsenisbnstore.com/

Canada: Library & Archives Canada
https://www.bac-lac.gc.ca/eng/services/isbn-canada/Pages/isbn-canada.aspx

Australia: Thorpe-Bowker
https://www.bowker.com/en/products-services/isbn-au/

What will it cost?

Depending on your country, you may not have to pay anything for your official ISBNs. Or you may have to spend quite a bit. If your country requires you to purchase ISBNs, the "free" ISBNs offered by the self-publishing platforms can look very tempting. But the "free" ones have some downsides.

#_____ ISBNs for your book (from Page 161)
X $_____ ISBN cost in your country
_____

$_____ ISBN cost for your book. *
*some services will allow for a bundle or package where you get multiple ISBNs for a discount.
(For example, in the U.S., Bowker offers one ISBN for $125 while ten ISBNs cost $295.)

Should you purchase these ISBNs at all?

Depending on your budget and the expected cost, you may be ready to get those "free" ISBNs. Let's walk through some questions first to see if that is the best option for your book and your vision. I put "free" in quotes because while self-publishing platforms offer these ISBNs to authors at no cost, they usually cannot be used on any other platform. So, if you get a "free" ISBN for your paperback book on Amazon, you cannot use that same ISBN to get your book wide distribution on IngramSpark.

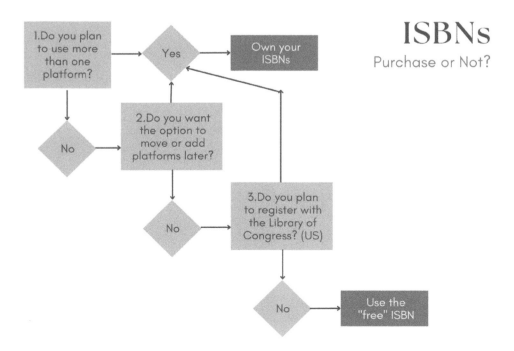

ISBNs
Purchase or Not?

1. Do you plan to use more than one self-publishing platform for your book?
    ❏ Yes   ❏ No

2. Do you want the option to move your book to additional platforms as they become available or as self-publishing changes?
    ❏ Yes   ❏ No

3. Do you want complete control over the metadata for your ISBN?
    ❏ Yes   ❏ No

4. Do you want to keep track of this information and manage your account with the ISBN agency for your country?
    ❏ Yes   ❏ No

5. Do you plan to register with the Library of Congress (Page 165)?
    ❏ Yes   ❏ No

I can't tell you which answers are right or wrong because there are no wrong answers. Depending on your strategy, you may elect to own your ISBNs (I do). Or you may decide that it isn't for you (e.g., because you know you will only ever do Kindle Select).

WHEN DO I NEED A NEW ISBN?

You need one ISBN for each format of your book. One for eBook, one for paperback, and one for hardcover. But if it's been a few years since you first published, and you have some edits to make to the interior text and a new cover for the book. What now? If you have created a new edition, you need a new ISBN. One for each format.

I have a separate checklist entirely dedicated to second editions. Self-Publishing Second Editions is available on my website. Use code WORKBOOK50 for 50% off.

My advice has always been to own your ISBNs. You are taking all this time and effort to write and self-publish this book, and you will let someone else own the ISBN? When I started out and had a super lean budget, I still paid to own my ISBNs. I'm so glad I did because if and when I want to move my titles to another platform, I can do so without issue.

OWN YOUR ISBNs?   ❏ Yes   ❏ No

If yes, complete the next Page 164
If no, skip to Page 165

Acquiring and Assigning ISBN Data

⏳ **When To Tackle**

At least six weeks before submitting for formatting if you also plan to apply for a Library of Congress Control Number (LCCN).

- ☐ Sign up for an account with the ISBN agency for your country.
- ☐ Complete account information.
- ☐ Purchase ISBNs when applicable.
- ☐ Input Book Metadata at least 48 hours before uploading. Need this to be assigned BEFORE doing your Library of Congress Control Number (LCCN) application. Metadata includes:
  - ○ Title, Subtitle, Edition
  - ○ Cover
  - ○ Author(s), Contributors
  - ○ Copyright year
  - ○ Language
  - ○ Format
  - ○ BISAC Categories (Page 175)
  - ○ Pricing, Availability Information.
- ☐ Add to the copyright page for the correct format.
  - ○ eBook ISBN
  - ○ Paperback ISBN
  - ○ Hardcover ISBN
  - ○ Audiobook ISBN
- ☐ **PUBLICATION DAY**: Update title status from forthcoming to active with your ISBN registration service or agency.

LCCN

The LCCN is the **Library of Congress Control Number**. This registration number will uniquely identify your book within the U.S. Library of Congress. There is no cost to acquiring this number, but there is a waiting period since it is the government.

If you aim to have your book in local libraries in the U.S., you should register for this number and have it on your copyright page. This will be tricky if you are electing an Amazon Exclusive strategy where you are NOT purchasing an ISBN. You need to know your ISBN to register your LCCN, but you won't get that "free" ISBN until your book is published. Also, many libraries do not acquire books from Amazon if they are out of their approved procurement process.

Acquiring and Assigning LCCN

⏳ When To Tackle

At least six weeks before submitting for formatting.

- ☐ Sign up for an account with the Library of Congress (LOC).
- ☐ Complete account information.
- ☐ Wait for the confirmation email that your account has been set up.
- ☐ Log in and begin a "Request."
- ☐ Input Book Metadata:
  - Title, Subtitle, Edition
  - Author(s), Contributors
  - Copyright year
  - Language
  - Format
  - BISAC Categories (Page 175)
  - ISBNs
  - Book Description

> **PRO TIP**
>
> I like to assign my ISBNs as I am applying for my LCCN, so I have that information pulled up on another screen.

- ☐ Submit the application. You will receive a confirmation email that the application was received.
- ☐ Within one to six weeks, the LCCN will come in.
- ☐ Add to the copyright page for the correct format. (Page 167, also see the copyright page for this book!)
- ☐ Add LCCN to ISBN metadata.
- ☐ Mail print copy of the book to LOC per requirement. If you don't have a print book version, don't send anything.

Copyright Registration

DISCLAIMER REMINDER
I am not a lawyer and if you have concerns about your copyright or any claims against it, consult with a lawyer.

In the U.S., your creative work is protected under copyright law the moment you create it. The copyright registration with the U.S. Copyright Office is an added layer of protection. It shows that as of this day and this time, this is the content of my work, so if anyone says identical content created after this date is theirs, they are in the wrong. **If you are based in another country, please reference your copyright law (and a lawyer!).**

As of October 2022, the registration fee is $65. This may be within your budget or out of it. Make this decision based on what works for you. You can apply when you publish the book or wait until you earn enough royalties to apply.

Acquiring and Assigning Copyright Registration

⧗ When To Tackle

On **Publication Day**.

PRO TIP

I like to apply on publication day. There can be added fees for applying ahead of publication day for express processing.

- ☐ Sign up for an account with the U.S. Copyright Office.
- ☐ Complete account information.
- ☐ Wait for a confirmation email that your account has been set up.
- ☐ Log in and "Register a Work."
- ☐ Input Book Metadata:
  - ○ Title, Subtitle, Edition
  - ○ Author(s), Contributors
  - ○ Copyright year
  - ○ Language
  - ○ Format
  - ○ ISBNs

If you find that your work has been pirated online, you will need to fill out a DMCA Takedown request. I review the process in my video on "Reporting Copyright Infringement."

- ☐ Submit the application. You will receive a confirmation email that the application was received.
- ☐ Within three to six months, the copyright registration will come in.
- ☐ Save this document with your other important items (passport, birth certificates, etc.).

Copyright Page

Every book must have a copyright page. Whether you elect to register your copyright for added protection or not, your book will have a copyright page. This book has one (go and flip back to the very beginning to see it).

The copyright page is immediately after your title page. This is the page where you are asserting your copyright and reserving your rights. You will specify where someone can contact you (the publisher) for any permissions. You will also include credit for your designers on this page.

Elements of your copyright page:

- ❏ Copyright Mark © + Year
- ❏ Copyright Holder: Is it you, your pen name, or your LLC?
- ❏ All Rights Reserved Disclaimer
- ❏ Content Disclaimer (use the applicable disclaimer(s) for your book, leave the rest)
  - ○ All Persons Fictitious for Fiction
  - ○ Not legal, accounting, financial, or medical advice for Non-Fiction
  - ○ U.S. Military Active Duty and Retired D.O.D. Disclaimer
  - ○ Link Disclaimer if you have affiliate links in the book
- ❏ ISBN Number (for that specific format or include ISBNs for all formats)
- ❏ LCCN Number
- ❏ Printed by...
- ❏ Cover Design Credit
- ❏ Cover Art Elements Credit
- ❏ Interior Design Credit
- ❏ Edition Number
- ❏ Website/ Location where people can request permission

COPYRIGHT PAGE RESOURCES

I use a template for each of my books. For authors who write in genres I don't have any experience with, I always recommend the Kindlepreneur Blog with Book Copyright Pages.

⏳ When To Tackle

Complete the copyright page and make sure it is included in the final draft prior to submitting for formatting.

EDITORS ON THE COPYRIGHT PAGE?

Some authors will also credit their editors on the copyright page. Some will give them a thank you in the acknowledgments section of the book. Some won't mention the editor at all. What is the right thing to do?

Ask your editor!

Some editors want to be included on the copyright page. Some don't. Why not? Well, just because they gave you a suggestion doesn't mean you took it. They may not always want their name on a book they edited if the author is stubborn and refuses to make the edits. Always ask first to ensure the editor wants their information on the book. Most will say yes, but it is always best to ask first.

Barcodes

The most important thing to remember when you are working through this page is that:

BARCODES ARE NOT ISBNS. ISBNS ARE NOT BARCODES!

First, let's make sure you even need to work through this exercise:

1. Are you planning to have print formats for your book?
    A. No – Jump to Page 171.
    B. Yes – See next question.

2. Are you planning to pursue a Brick-and-Mortar strategy? (Refer back to Page 68.)
    A. No – Jump to Page 171.
    B. Yes – Work through this exercise.

> **WHY DOES BRICK-AND-MORTAR MATTER?**
>
> If you are pursuing a Brick-and-Mortar strategy, your barcode should have the retail price. This makes it easier for the bookstore. Without Brick-and-Mortar, you can forgo a price on the back, making it easier to change the price later.

You only need barcodes for any physical products you create. For your book, that would be the paperback and hardcover editions. If you elected to do physical CDs for your audiobook, you would also need a barcode, but most audiobooks are digital files now, which do not need a barcode. You will need a barcode for each physical format of your book.

Acquiring and Assigning Barcodes

You have several options for acquiring a barcode:

1. You can acquire one from the same service that provided your ISBN.
   In the U.S., for example, this is also through Bowker. There is a $25 charge for a barcode.

2. You can use the free barcode assigned by your self-publishing print-on-demand service.
   These barcodes are applied when the print files are processed. No price is included on the barcode. If you have a barcode with the price on the cover, you can indicate that so the platform does not place a new one on top of it.

3. You can use a low cost or free barcode generator.
   In some cases, these allow you to add a price. In others, they do not. Some are free; others ask for a small donation to keep their website running. You want an EAN ISBN Barcode that will show both the price and the ISBN.

⧖ When To Tackle

Before you finalize the print cover with your designer. This can be the day before, or it can be the month before. But once you set the barcode up, you're locked in.

AN IMPORTANT NOTE

You must know the price you want to charge (and have confirmed the royalty) before you assign your barcodes with a price. Once the price is assigned, you cannot change it. If you need to change the price, you need to acquire a new barcode and have it switched out on the cover. Ensure you have priced your book accordingly to account for rising costs, but not enough to lose the sale.

M.K.'S STRATEGY

I own all of my ISBNs. I have from the outset. As I've added new platforms to my mix, this was a huge timesaver. I also apply for a Library of Congress Control Number for all of my books. It's free and gives me the ability to see my books in libraries.

As for barcodes, in some cases I have used a barcode with the price. When I was marketing some of my science fiction books to local bookstores this was a big plus. For other books where I have no plans to promote them to brick-and-mortar stores, I use the free barcode from the platform that has no price on it. I can always change my covers later to include a barcode with a price on it if I really want to.

SECTION END:

After working through all the checklists in this section, you should have the following:

❏ Decision on whether or not you will own your ISBNs or use a "free" one from a self-publishing platform.
❏ Total number of ISBNs you will need for your book.
❏ Library of Congress Number (for U.S. Authors).
❏ Decision on if you need a barcode for your book and if it has to have the price on it or not.
❏ Decision on whether to register your copyright now or later.

Fill in your important book information here and refer back when you are uploading.

Your Book				
Format	eBook	Paperback	Hardcover	Audiobook
Price				
Barcodes (if applicable)	N/A			N/A
ISBNs				
LCCN				
Copyright Registration				

BOOK DESCRIPTIONS, CATEGORIES, AND KEYWORDS

Every author laments the dreaded book description or blurb. How can you condense hundreds of pages of perfect words into two paragraphs?

Well, you have to, and it's critical, as you'll see in the following pages.

First, you need to be able to describe your book, so people know what it is about. Otherwise, why should they spend their time (and money) on it? Second, the self-publishing platforms need to understand how to categorize it. Yes, you will tell them the exact categories in which you want to be placed, but the text of your description and the book itself will help the algorithm further. If you want your book to be discovered, this section is critical.

This is a delicate balance where you will need to write for the reader, but you want the systems to be happy too. Through this section, we'll work on our description and infuse it with the categories and keywords in a way that makes sense to a human, not a robot.

⧗ When To Tackle

In between editing rounds or as you are drafting when your creative juices for the content are tapped. Ideally, this needs to be DONE by the time you send the creative brief to your cover artist because the book description will likely go on the back of the book.

Amazon Categories

For starters, let's address Amazon Categories. In the larger sense, you are defining your genre and sub-genre here. But Amazon has its own unique list of hundreds of categories. They have products in every potential consumer market, so their categories get very specific. They can also change and add more as book trends change and new sub-genres emerge.

Let's start at the Amazon.com Homepage and start to find your categories. You likely already have a big-picture idea like Fantasy or Personal Finance. Once you navigate to this larger category, you will see more options pop up – these are sub-categories. We want to drill down as far as possible.

> For Amazon KDP, you will input your top two categories when uploading. You can add up to ten (if you can find that many to request) via Author Central once the book is approved. If you can't find ten perfect categories, **don't force any that don't make sense.**

You will need to record the FULL categories string (examples below), and you will want to do this for the eBook and print. You can do this on Audible.com for your ACX listing. You will provide these strings when you request more via Author Central. (We will go over Amazon Author Central on Page 272)

Here is an example of a full category string:

Books> Science Fiction & Fantasy > Science Fiction > Time Travel

Kindle Store > Kindle eBooks> Business & Money > Personal Finance > Budgeting & Money Management > Budgeting

Two Stores / One Website

Amazon.com has two "stores" for books. One is for eBooks on their Kindle Store. The other is for print books in their Books category. If you are uploading your book as both an eBook and a print book on Amazon KDP, you will need to find categories for both "stores" within Amazon.com.

Kindle Store Categories:

1) _____

2) _____

3) _____

4) _____

5) _____

6) _____

7) _____

8) _____

9) _____

10) _____

Book Categories:

1) _____

2) _____

3) _____

4) _____

5) _____

6) _____

7) _____

8) _____

9) _____

10) _____

ACX Audiobook Categories:

1) _____

2) _____

3) _____

> ▶ I updated my book categories on Amazon after a few years, which made a big difference in how my book was ranked. Don't sleep on this metadata for your book!

BISAC Categories

To the rest of the book world, there is a set list of standard categories. These are BISAC (Book Industry Standard and Communications) codes set by the Book Industry Study Group (BISG). With the other self-publishing platforms, you can select three BISAC categories your book best fits into. It can help to look at these ahead of time, but each platform will have a drop-down to choose from.

BISAC Codes:

1) _____

2) _____

3) _____

Keywords

Distinct from categories are keywords. While you may use the exact sub-category as a keyword, you usually have more space here to describe your book exactly. This is how the platforms will know what your book is about. Is it a friends-to-lovers romance? Is it a keto cookbook? You may have those words in the description, but this is where you can tell your platform's algorithm exactly how to index or categorize your book.

But you can't wholly tailor these to a computer. You need to anticipate how your ideal reader will search for books. Think of it this way: your book will pop up when someone searches for "XYZ" term on Amazon or Barnes & Noble. "Best Book Ever!" is not a keyword you should ever use. But how about a "step by step guide to self-publishing"? Or "complete checklist to self-publish your book." Those might work.

Take your time and remember that you can and should optimize this. Some experts say to update the keywords every 30 days, others 90 days. If you are busy, look at them at least once a year.

You get to pick seven keywords or keyword phrases to input into KDP, and other platforms have a character limit. Let's start with a broad list and narrow it down:

- ❏ Create a list of keywords you think might fit.
- ❏ Open an incognito browser and go to the Amazon Books and Amazon Kindle Store. Input your initial keywords, and then see what auto-fills for additional ideas.
- ❏ Pick keywords with a good number of books showing: 1,000-10,000. If only a few books show, then it is too niche. If hundreds of thousands show, the keyword is not specific enough.
- ❏ Look at those top books and see what categories those books are in. (Revise your category list on Page 174 as needed.)

Potential Book Keywords

1) _____

2) _____

3) _____

4) _____

5) _____

6) _____

7) _____

8) _____

9) _____

10) _____

11) _____

12) _____

13) _____

14) _____

15) _____

16) _____

17) _____

18) _____

19) _____

20) _____

21) _____

22) _____

23) _____

24) _____

25) _____

26) _____

27) _____

28) _____

29) _____

30) _____

31) _____

32) _____

33) _____

34) _____

35) _____

36) _____

37) _____

38) _____

39) _____

40) _____

41) _____

42) _____

43) _____

44) _____

45) _____

46) _____

47) _____

48) _____

49) _____

50) _____

Remember:

- Long-tail keywords that best describe the book can be very helpful.
- Any keywords you select when uploading can be switched out later for alternates on your list.

Selected Book Keywords

1) _____

2) _____

3) _____

4) _____

5) _____

6) _____

7) _____

Book Description

Unless you have editorial quotes from a dozen reputable newspapers and acclaimed authors, you will likely put your book description on the back of your book (see Pages 184-190). This copy will also go on your book's page on any retailers and review platforms. This description can be a chapter-by-chapter bullet-point outline of what the reader will learn if you are writing non-fiction. For fiction, it can be a short and mysterious paragraph that will leave the reader wanting more.

After you have caught the eye of the reader with your cover, they will read your book description to see if this is something they want to pick up. Spend some time looking at the descriptions of books in your genre. Do they start with a one-sentence headline or hook? Do they list out the action items from the how-to book? Are there only four lines on the plot, and the rest of the description compares the book to others in the genre?

Use these other descriptions as research and craft several versions of your own. Always have someone else read or proofread your description. This can be your editor or a friend. Nothing is more embarrassing than when you put all your effort into the book to have someone comment that there is a typo in the first line of your book description. (I learned that one the hard way, so you don't have to.) One tactic you can use is to craft a few options and let your friends select the one they would take action on. You may still have to optimize the text over time, but it will give you a solid place to start.

(As with other elements of the book process, you can hire someone to write your book description. Sometimes this can be as inexpensive as $15-$25 on Fiverr. Or you could spend up to $200. If it is in your budget, why not? If it isn't in your budget, write your own.)

Book Description Exercise

Try to distill your book description into one sentence, then one word. This one word should be the theme of your entire description. Here is an example from my first book, *Nailbiters*:

One Sentence Description: "Can Dora survive the invasion with her humanity intact?"

Drilling it Down: "Survive the invasion."

One Word: "Survive"

From there I can rebuild the description back up:

"As the invasion begins, we all scatter like insects when the lights turn on. *Nailbiters* is not a post-apocalyptic tale, it is apocalyptic. It follows Dora as the world begins to end, and society crumbles.

Nailbiters is a story of survival. The first in a hard science fiction series, this story will keep you up at night.

On the morning of the invasion, Dora takes off running. She lasts three weeks before she is captured. Follow her story from the open plains of Texas to the desert of California. Readers have called this technothriller "chilling" and "visceral." Find out why they haven't been able to put it down.

Can Dora survive the invasion with her humanity intact? Read *Nailbiters* today to find out."

Now you get to try this for your book:

One Sentence Description: _____

Drilling it Down: _____

One Word: _____

Book Description Draft 1:

_____

_____

_____

_____

_____

_____

Now that you have a starting point reference your top selected categories (Page 174) and keywords (Page 176) and see if there is a way to organically and naturally mention them in the description.

Book Description Draft 2:

_____

_____

_____

_____

_____

_____

_____

_____

_____

_____

_____

_____

_____

_____

_____

_____

_____

_____

_____

Revise and rework your description every few months. If you can't commit to that frequency, at least revisit it once a year. Each time you should start fresh – don't look at your current description. You'll find that you have more to work with each time you revisit this important element of your book marketing strategy.

SECTION END:

After working through all the exercises in this section, you should have the following:

- ☐ List of Amazon categories you will input when uploading your book.
- ☐ List of Amazon categories you will request for your listing after publishing.
- ☐ List of BISAC categories for your book.
- ☐ List of keywords for your book.
- ☐ Rich book description that contains keywords and categories.

BLURBS AND EDITORIAL REVIEWS

This could (maybe should) be in the marketing section, but it is here because you MAY also use this for your book cover. (Remember my sweet Venn diagram about how we have to do many different things at once?)

Let's first define Blurbs and Editorial Reviews:

Blurbs: A short review from an author or expert in your book's genre praising the book and recommending it to readers. These are often seen on the front and back cover of books.

Editorial Reviews: A review of your book from a publication or respected book review service (e.g., New York Times Review of Books or Kirkus Reviews). These are often seen on the front and back cover of books. You may have to pay a reading fee for some of these services. Because they are known to provide fair and honest reviews, these reviews are allowed in the editorial review section of your book's retail page on Amazon.com, BarnesandNoble.com, and the like. Usually, you are provided, or can shorten to, a few brief sentences for marketing purposes.

Blurbs and Editorial Reviews go in the "Editorial Reviews" section of your book's metadata.

These are both completely optional. *Having these does not guarantee the success of your book*, but it can be one element in your larger marketing and promotional strategy.

⧗ When To Tackle

When your book is in the final copy edit or before you send it to formatting. It is okay to ask for a review at this stage – many authors and review services know that you will want to use a review on the cover, and they know that it takes time.

Blurbs

First, let's aim for some Blurbs. These will likely be at no cost to you except for any social capital you have with these authors and experts. You should also send them an autographed copy of the book once it is printed as a thank you. (It also helps to remind them to promote the book!)

Before you ask, you first need to identify WHO you will ask. Think of this as your college application list. You have a "Dream" Blurb – the #1 person you want to rave about your book. Then you have your "Reach" Blurbs – you would still be very excited to have these people review and praise your book. Then your "Safety" Blurbs – the author friends you know will be happy to support you.

Let's list and identify them now:

DREAM BLURB

_____

REACH BLURBS

_____

_____

_____

SAFETY BLURBS

_____

_____

_____

_____

_____

_____

_____

You have space to identify six Safety Blurbs. Because you should have a maximum of six Blurbs. There is only so much real estate on your back cover. If you ask 20 people to give you a blurb and all 20 people provide one, you will be in a world of trouble deciding who makes the cut and who doesn't.

For this reason, you should reach out to your Dream Blurb first. Based on their response, your Reach Blurbs, then to your Safety squad. Remember, you are reasonably sure everyone on your Safety Blurb list will say yes. Only ask the number of people whose Blurbs you can fit on the back of the book!

Once you know WHO you will ask, you can craft your request email. This should be short and sweet. It should tell the person who you are, what your book is about, and make a direct ask for them to read it and provide a blurb by a specific date.

DO NOT ATTACH THE BOOK TO THIS FIRST EMAIL!
ONLY SEND THE MANUSCRIPT ONCE THEY AGREE!

Name	Contact Information	Blurb Requested	Will Blurb? Yes / No	Manuscript Sent	Blurb Received	Thank You Sent

Now that you have your Blurbs, here is what you need to do with them:

- ❐ Create a Microsoft Word or Google Doc to list all the Blurbs.
- ❐ Format the Blurbs so each will look the same.
- ❐ Confirm with each person that they approve of the blurb and any formatting. (You may have to trim the length of their blurb or correct any grammar. Always get their approval.)
- ❐ Provide blurbs to the cover artist for the back cover. (See Page 196 or 203)
- ❐ **Upload Day + 2**: Add to the "Editorial Reviews" section in Amazon Author Central. (For other platforms, you can add these as you complete the upload process.)
- ❐ **PUBLICATION DAY - 4 Weeks**: Send an advance copy of the book to your blurb team with a thank you note.
- ❐ **PUBLICATION DAY:** Thank the blurb team and tag them on social media.
- ❐ POST PUBLICATION MARKETING: Leverage blurbs in continued messaging about the book.

BLURB FORMATTING EXAMPLES

"This book is amazing!" – Stephen King

This book is amazing! – Stephen King, Best-Selling Author

"This book is amazing!" – **Stephen King**, Author of *On Writing*

Editorial Reviews

Separate from Blurbs are Editorial Reviews. In a general sense, these are longer and more thoughtful reviews. An example would be a reviewer with a popular publication (say, The New York Times or The Wall Street Journal). Getting your book into the hands of people at major publications (or even small ones) can be a game of "who you know, not what you know."

There are several services that also offer editorial reviews. They charge a reading fee. These reviews are impartial. They usually have a bell curve of star ratings. Most fall in the middle, with a few books meriting their coveted higher-star rankings. Some services are specific to self-published or indie-published books. Some are specific to children's books.

Even a slam-dunk editorial review can be costly and not guarantee more sales. It can help. But it is all about how you leverage and promote that review.

Here is what you need to look at before you pay for anything:

- ❏ What is in your budget for this form of marketing?
- ❏ Could this budget be allocated elsewhere?
- ❏ Is this reviewer legitimate and credible? (Research first!)
- ❏ What is their estimated turnaround time? Will I be able to add this to my cover? Am I okay delaying my cover so I can put this on it?

NOTE: If the service gives your book a three-star rating or lower, they usually give you the option not to have it published. They are not out to tank your book, but you are still out your reading fee.

Service	Fee	Turnaround Time	Notes	Will you use this service? Yes / No

IF you elect to go with one of these services AND you get a four-star review or higher, here is what to do with it:

- ❏ Provide the shortened review to the cover designer. (See Page 196 or 203)
- ❏ **Upload Day + 2**: Add to the "Editorial Reviews" section in Amazon Author Central. (For other platforms, you can add these as you complete the upload process.)
- ❏ POST PUBLICATION MARKETING: Leverage editorial reviews in continued messaging about the book.

COVER DESIGN AND FORMATTING

The design of your book, interior and exterior, is just as important as the text itself. Yes, people do judge a book by its cover. It is often the very first thing they judge about it. And the interior needs to look good too. This doesn't mean an overly designed expensive project, but it should be legible and easy to read in any format. This section will review your options for both the cover design and formatting and help you select the best options for your book.

If you are aiming to write and self-publish a children's book, then the design is much more important to you than to a novelist who will have little to no images in their book. There are exercises at the end of this section on Page 220 specific to children's books. Please refer to this section for the appropriate lists and decision exercises.

TECH-SAVVY

how hard is this step?

hard – requires tech skills
& patience!

easy – most every author
can tackle on their own

For those considering the cover design and formatting themselves to save money, note this requires technical skill and practice within the appropriate design programs and an eye for design. Hiring a professional to help with this step is okay and often encouraged. There are many low-cost, high-quality options for self-publishing authors.

When To Tackle

The timing here is a balancing act. Some say to get your cover designed the second you think of your book, so you have it done, and it can inspire you to finish writing. Others leave it to the last second, as cover ideas will percolate as you write the book. I think you are best served to get your cover done during some of your final editing rounds. Many designers will be booked up weeks in advance, so you will want to research and lock in your design team before the final edits are done; otherwise, you are waiting for the work to begin.

Cover Inspiration

For starters, I suggest looking at book covers that you find appealing. You're already reading books in the genre that you write because you A) like that genre and B) are researching your genre. I like to use Pinterest to save cover concepts and designs I like. You can also create a custom list on Goodreads of your favorite covers. Just set up a place to save them. No matter who designs the cover, you should be saving ideas in one location.

Pick one of these methods or come up with your own.

- ❐ Create a Pinterest board for cover art ideas.
- ❐ Create a custom Goodreads list of book covers you like.
- ❐ Create a folder on your computer for book covers you like.

What gets saved:

- ❐ Book covers you like.
- ❐ Book covers you do not like (in a separate sub-folder or board).
- ❐ Book cover elements you like (focus on the spine and back cover as well).
- ❐ Design elements on items that are not books.
- ❐ Cover images of books you want readers to rank you next to.

Who Will Design the Cover?

It is time to decide WHO will create your beautiful cover. You have some branching options here. First, you must determine if you will go the DIY (do-it-yourself) route or hire someone to design the cover. If you are considering designing the cover yourself, follow these questions to determine if this is the best route for you and what you need to do next. If you already know you want to hire a designer, skip to Page 198.

Circle the answer to each question below, Yes or No

	Yes	No
Do you have any design experience?	1	2
Will you use photoshop or a professional design software?	1	2
Will you use a free online design software?	1	2
Do you plan to use any images or design elements that another designer or artist created?	1	2

Tally up the answers. If you have a five or less, perhaps you will do well with the DIY Cover Design method. If you scored above five, I strongly suggest you work with a professional. If the extent of your design experience is an online free design program (like Canva, Pexels, Pixlr, among others), I can almost guarantee you will want to throw your computer at some point in this process. Also, many of the designs on Canva are not eligible to be used as a book cover unless you pay for a template or upgrade to their paid version. There is no such thing as a beautiful free cover. You either need to pay for design software or pay with your time to learn the software and book cover design basics.

Referring to our technical difficulty scale, designing your own cover is hard. It is doable, but I would only recommend those with design software experience and an abundance of patience try this route

TECH-SAVVY

how hard is this step?

hard – requires tech skills
& patience!

easy – most every author
can tackle on their own

Final Decision

- ❑ DIY Cover
- ❑ Professionally Designed Cover

DIY Cover Checklist

If you have decided to create your own cover, then you will need to follow these steps.

Refer to Page 50 to confirm which formats you will need a cover file for. Cross out any formats from the list below that you will NOT be using.

Remember that you should consider what goes on the spine of your print book and the text for the back cover. (Pages 182 and 185– Book Descriptions and Blurbs)

Each self-publishing platform has a file creation guide that will tell you in "design speak" the file type, color settings, and other details for your cover file. They will also have a cover template generator. I ALWAYS suggest that you use the template when submitting your final files.

Concept

- ☐ Book cover design concept brainstorming.
- ☐ Book cover design options created.
- ☐ Review two or three cover design options.

I have videos showing you how to adjust your cover files for Amazon KDP and IngramSpark on my channel. You can follow along.

Feedback

- ☐ Get feedback on two or three options. (This can be your support team or other authors. You could post a poll on social media. Ideally, you want feedback from someone who reads in your genre. I would suggest not telling them you designed the cover. They will withhold their honest opinion to spare your feelings if you tell them you designed it. Tell them the concepts are back from your "designer.")
- ☐ Revise the top design option.

eBook Cover

- ☐ Lock in the eBook front cover.
- ☐ Save the eBook cover working file as a PSD.
- ☐ Save the eBook cover as a JPEG.

Paperback Cover

- ❏ Create a new file for the paperback print cover ("Save As" a new file).
- ❏ Download the paperback print cover template from ALL platforms you will upload to.
- ❏ Save the paperback print templates and confirm the dimensions for each platform.
- ❏ Expand the canvas dimensions to match the paperback print cover file template specifications.
- ❏ Save the paperback print cover working file as a PSD. This is the master file you will use and adapt as needed for each platform. You can save a working file for each platform, but changes to the cover must be made on multiple files.
- ❏ Export the paperback print covers for each platform. Save each file as a PDF.

Hardcover Files

- ❏ Create a new file for the hardcover print cover ("Save As" new file).
- ❏ Save the hardcover print templates and confirm the dimensions for each platform.
- ❏ Expand the canvas dimensions to match the hardcover print cover file template specifications.
- ❏ Save the hardcover print cover working file as a PSD.
- ❏ Export the hardcover print cover for each platform. Save each file as a PDF

Audiobook Cover

- ❏ Create a new file for the audiobook cover ("Save As" new file from your eBook working file).
- ❏ Expand the canvas dimensions to match the audiobook cover specifications.
- ❏ Save the audiobook cover working file as a PSD.
- ❏ Export the audiobook cover for each platform as a PNG and a JPEG.

FINAL FILES SAVED LIST:

- ❏ eBook Cover
- ❏ Paperback Cover
- ❏ Hardcover Case
- ❏ Hardcover Jacket
- ❏ Audiobook Cover

HIRING A COVER DESIGNER

If looking through the last few pages hurt your brain, I don't blame you. Designing a book cover is an art and a science. You're already working on writing the best book possible. Let's hire a pro to handle your book cover. But the question is: who is the best for your book? Let's work through these steps to find the best designer.

Where to find a great designer: You should use one or all of these options to find different designers or design services to work with. Keep in mind that longer lists are harder to whittle down. Right now, we are looking at making a list of potential designers. We will eliminate some options next.

- ❐ Pick out your favorite two or three book covers from your inspiration board. Check the copyright page to confirm who designed it. Search for their name online and jot down their contact information.
- ❐ Search for Book Cover Design on Fiverr. Check the reviews and only add designers to your list whose style you like.
- ❐ Search for Book Cover Design on Reedsy. Check the reviews and only add designers to your list whose style you like.
- ❐ Search for Book Cover Design on 99Designs. Check the reviews and only add designers to your list whose style you like.
- ❐ Look at pricing for The Works from Formatted Books.
- ❐ Look at pricing for Cover Design Packages from 100Covers.
- ❐ Ask other indie authors for recommendations or check the copyright page for the design credit.

Where to NOT find a great designer: Don't just ask a friend who happens to have photoshop on their computer to design your book cover. Do they have experience designing book covers? Do they know the upload requirements for your platforms? Maybe they offered to help you out for free, but if you don't like the design (or if it is constantly rejected from each platform), are you willing to tell them "thanks, no thanks"?

VETTING POTENTIAL DESIGNERS

It is essential to ask questions at this stage. You will be able to whittle down your list quickly as you find out who is in and out of your price range, who has the experience to help, and who communicates with you. A few critical items to consider:

- What is included in the price? Are you just getting an eBook cover? If you need other formats, what will that cost? Refer back to Page 50 to your list of formats. They may include some additional promotional designs too. This isn't necessary but can be a bonus.

- Will any added costs be passed on to you if the designer licenses images for their work?

- How many rounds of revisions are included? What is the added cost for additional rounds?

- What is their current turnaround time on projects? When can they start?

- We will also discuss formatting in the next section, but can this designer do that too? Having one designer to work with could be a big time and energy savings.

- Do they have experience with self-published books or traditionally published books? The designer will know book design, but if they have only worked on traditionally published books, they will likely charge more and need you to provide the platform cover templates to drop the design into.

- Can they do illustrations? Illustrating is different from designing. If you want illustrated elements, you will need to ensure they can do that.

- How do they communicate? What questions are they asking you? Do you think you will mesh well?

You will find a chart comparing your design options on the following pages. I have already input Formatted Books and 100Covers. I have worked with both of these services as well as individual designers. These services should be part of your mix when considering who to work with. Maybe you elect to go with someone else, but keep them in the mix to start.

Comparing Design Options

Designer	Contact Info	Quoted Price	Experience with Self-Published Books?	What is included in the project? (Compare against what you need)	Number of Design Rounds	Estimated Timeline for Final Files
Formatted Books	https://formattedbooks.com/?ref=31		YES	☐ Ebook cover ☐ Paperback cover ☐ Hardcover – case laminate ☐ Hardcover – jacket ☐ Audiobook cover ☐ Social media graphics ☐ A+ Content ☐ Interior Formatting too?		
100Covers	http://100covers.com/?ref=49		YES	☐ Ebook cover ☐ Paperback cover ☐ Hardcover – case laminate ☐ Hardcover – jacket ☐ Audiobook cover ☐ Social media graphics ☐ A+ Content ☐ Interior Formatting too?		
				☐ Ebook cover ☐ Paperback cover ☐ Hardcover – case laminate ☐ Hardcover – jacket ☐ Audiobook cover ☐ Social media graphics ☐ A+ Content ☐ Interior Formatting too?		

Designer	Contact Info	Quoted Price	Experience with Self-Published Books?	What is included in the project? (Compare against what you need)	Number of Design Rounds	Estimated Timeline for Final Files
				☐ Ebook cover ☐ Paperback cover ☐ Hardcover – case laminate ☐ Hardcover – jacket ☐ Audiobook cover ☐ Social media graphics ☐ A+ Content ☐ Interior Formatting too?		
				☐ Ebook cover ☐ Paperback cover ☐ Hardcover – case laminate ☐ Hardcover – jacket ☐ Audiobook cover ☐ Social media graphics ☐ A+ Content ☐ Interior Formatting too?		
				☐ Ebook cover ☐ Paperback cover ☐ Hardcover – case laminate ☐ Hardcover – jacket ☐ Audiobook cover ☐ Social media graphics ☐ A+ Content ☐ Interior Formatting too?		

Designer	Contact Info	Quoted Price	Experience with Self-Published Books?	What is included in the project? (Compare against what you need)	Number of Design Rounds	Estimated Timeline for Final Files
				☐ Ebook cover ☐ Paperback cover ☐ Hardcover – case laminate ☐ Hardcover – jacket ☐ Audiobook cover ☐ Social media graphics ☐ A+ Content ☐ Interior Formatting too?		
				☐ Ebook cover ☐ Paperback cover ☐ Hardcover – case laminate ☐ Hardcover – jacket ☐ Audiobook cover ☐ Social media graphics ☐ A+ Content ☐ Interior Formatting too?		
				☐ Ebook cover ☐ Paperback cover ☐ Hardcover – case laminate ☐ Hardcover – jacket ☐ Audiobook cover ☐ Social media graphics ☐ A+ Content ☐ Interior Formatting too?		

Professional Cover Checklist

Now that you have decided which designer or design service to use, this is the checklist to follow to ensure your covers are completed.

Refer to Page 50 to confirm which formats you will need a cover file for. Cross out any formats from the list below that you will NOT be using.

Remember that you should consider what goes on the spine of your print book and the text for the back cover as well. (Pages 182 and 185– Book Descriptions and Blurbs):

Research/Hiring

- ❏ Research potential designers (Pages 200-202).
- ❏ Whittle down the list to the top two or three.
- ❏ Select your top designer.
- ❏ Pay for services.
- ❏ Provide design brief. (Description of your book, books you want to compare to, desired categories, book covers you do/do not like.)

> Some designers will ask for the entire design fee upfront. Others will do a down payment/ final payment set-up. Typically design services ask for the entire payment upfront. If you are working with an individual designer, you may be able to make multiple payments.

Concept and Feedback

- ❏ Review two or three cover design options.
- ❏ Get feedback on two or three options. (This can be your support team or other authors. You could post a poll on social media. Ideally, you want feedback from someone who reads in your genre.)
- ❏ Provide feedback to the designer on which one you like and what elements you do/do not like.
- ❏ Review the next round. *CONFIRM YOU ARE NOT GOING OVER ON DESIGN ROUNDS*

> Designers have all gone through rigorous training and critiques. If you don't like the first concepts, be specific. What do you not like? What did you expect but not see? They are designers, not mind-readers.

eBook Cover

- ❏ Lock in the eBook front cover.
- ❏ Save the eBook cover file.

Paperback Cover

- ❒ Provide spine and back cover text.
- ❒ Provide the final interior page count so they can set the spine width.
- ❒ Provide confirmed interior trim size. (Page 46)
- ❒ Review design with text.
- ❒ Provide feedback and edits.
- ❒ Lock in the paperback cover file.
- ❒ Save the paperback cover file.

Each self-publishing platform has a file creation guide that will tell you in "design speak" the file type, color settings, and other details for your cover file. They will also have a cover template generator. If your designer is not experienced with self-published books, provide them with the cover template.

Hardcover Files

- ❒ Confirm text on the hardcover will match the paperback cover.
- ❒ If you will have a hardcover jacket, provide additional text for front and back flaps.
- ❒ Provide final interior page count (if different from paperback).
- ❒ Provide confirmed interior trim size (if different from paperback).
- ❒ Review design with text.
- ❒ Provide feedback and edits.
- ❒ Lock in the hardcover file.
- ❒ Save the hardcover file.

Even if you have purchased a pre-made book cover that is adapted to include your title and author name, you still need to ensure you have the different formats and files. Confirm with the designer what is included before you purchase the premade cover.

Audiobook Cover

- ❒ Confirm additional text for the audiobook cover file. ("Narrated by...")
- ❒ Lock in the audiobook cover design.
- ❒ Save the audiobook cover file.

Unsure if you'll even have an audiobook version of your book? Get the audiobook cover anyway if it is part of the package! It is easier to do it now than have to go back and ask for it later.

Design Extras *IF this is part of your design contract*

- ❏ Save social media graphics.
- ❏ Save A+ Content graphics. (Page 273)
- ❏ Save working files for the design.

FINAL FILES SAVED LIST:

- ❏ eBook Cover
- ❏ Paperback Cover
- ❏ Hardcover Case
- ❏ Hardcover Jacket
- ❏ Audiobook Cover
- ❏ Social Media Graphics
- ❏ A+ Content

Cover Reveal Planning

Your cover is the most prominent marketing element for your book. You may have seen many authors do a cover reveal where they hype up their audience about the final design. If you do this, you may forgo doing audience polls or surveys about the design concepts (since the final would be in the mix already). It means you may not be crowdsourcing feedback on the cover concept. That's okay. You don't have to leverage your social network for cover feedback. Perhaps you just ask a few close friends.

As a reminder, this is not a necessary element of your book launch strategy. But it is one thing you CAN do to build excitement for the book launch. One problem we often face as indie authors is that we have no control over when our book purchase links go live (we get 72-hour windows). Ideally, you want a link for people to pre-order or register their interest when you announce the cover. So, if you plan to reveal the cover and want to tease the announcement, you must remind people that the cover announcement is soon, while the links to purchase may already be live somewhere. Up to you how to proceed from a timing perspective.

If you plan to do a cover reveal, here are some planning elements to work through:

COVER REVEAL DATE: _____ (Potentially the same day as your pre-order launch or publication date)

-1 Day: _____ Final Teaser for the upcoming cover reveal

-5 Days: _____ First Teaser for the upcoming cover reveal

Will the cover reveal coincide with the pre-order launch/publication launch?
❏ Yes   ❏ No

Where will the cover be announced? Circle the platforms and rank them in order if you plan to announce to a select group first.

- ❏ ARC Reader List
- ❏ Newsletter List
- ❏ Facebook
- ❏ Twitter
- ❏ YouTube
- ❏ Instagram
- ❏ TikTok

Creative Assets: You may utilize some of these or all of them. Be sure you use the correct sizing dimensions for each planned platform.

- ☐ Cover reveal countdown image(s): Cover is obscured with some of it visible, date of reveal on the image.
- ☐ Cover reveal countdown video(s): Cover is obscured with some of it visible, date of reveal on the image.
- ☐ Cover reveal image(s): Cover is fully visible.
- ☐ Cover reveal video(s): Cover is fully visible.

Interior Formatting

Before you send your manuscript to be formatted, you need to make sure this is it, the FINAL copy! This is the most perfect manuscript you can make with NO changes to be made.

After all the edits and revisions, you are certain of every word, comma, and indentation. This is your **"speak now or forever hold your peace"** moment.

Below is a final checklist for ALL items that should be complete before you send your book for formatting.

BEFORE YOU SEND TO FORMATTING:

- ❒ Complete the final pass-through of the text. You should have done at least one round of reading the final manuscript out loud.
- ❒ Remove any notes/comments/track changes left over from editing rounds.
- ❒ Confirm you have a completed Copyright page. Your ISBN and LCCN are included if you plan to obtain those.
- ❒ Confirm you have a Table of Contents (formatter will add page numbers for the print edition, no page numbers for the eBook).
- ❒ Confirm you have your Bibliography.
- ❒ Confirm you have your Acknowledgements section.
- ❒ Confirm you have a Dedication.
- ❒ Confirm you have an end note with a way for readers to get more from you and subscribe or follow you.

Who Will Design the Interior?

It is time to decide WHO will format the interior of your book. This is very important because this is literally your manuscript becoming a book. You need to consider the different formats and how any elements translate to print or responsive eBooks.

You have some branching options here. First, you need to decide if you will go the DIY (do-it-yourself) route or hire someone to format the book. If you are considering formatting the book yourself, follow through with these questions to determine if this is the best route for you and what you need to do next. If you already know you want to hire a formatter (or you hired a designer who can do both interior and exterior), skip to Page 213.

Circle the answer to each question below, Yes or No

	Yes	No
Do you have any design experience?	1	2
Will you use InDesign or a professional design software?	1	2
Will you use a free online design software?	1	2
Will you use a writing and formatting software (ex. Scrivener or Atticus)	1	2
Do you plan to use any images or design elements that another designer or artist created?	1	2

Tally up the answers. You may do well with DIY formatting if you have a five or less. If you scored above five, I strongly suggest you work with a professional. If you don't have experience with formatting and don't have access to formatting software (InDesign, Scrivener, Atticus), you may be biting off more than you can chew. If you wrote your entire book in a word processor, it might be equally daunting to copy and paste it into software like Scrivener to do the formatting yourself. The more images or graphs you have, the more difficult it will be to format for you and your formatter, but at least a formatter has experience with this aspect.

Referring to our technical difficulty scale, designing your own cover is hard. It is doable, but I would only recommend those with design software experience and an abundance of patience try this route.

TECH-SAVVY

how hard is this step?

hard – requires tech skills & patience!

easy – most every author can tackle on their own

Remember, your time is precious. But if your budget is tight, you can still format the book yourself. You can purchase software that is specific to writing and formatting books, like:

- Vellum (Mac only)
- Scrivener
- Atticus

Or you can use formatting software that can be used for many different types of projects, including books:

- Adobe InDesign ($$$)
- Scribus (Free to download, takes time to learn)
- Calibre (Free to download, takes time to learn)

Final Decision

- ☐ DIY Formatting
- ☐ Professionally Formatted Book

DIY Formatting

If you have decided to format your own book, then you will need to follow these steps.

Refer back to Page 50 to confirm which formats you will need. Cross out any formats from the list below that you will NOT be using. I strongly suggest you **use one trim size for paperback and hardcover**, so you don't have to create two print interior files.

Formatting Software

- ☐ Review formatting software available to you.
- ☐ Compare pricing and features.
- ☐ Select software.
- ☐ Watch tutorial videos on how to use the software before you do any work.

Manuscript Locked

- ☐ SPEAK NOW OR HOLD YOUR PEACE.
- ☐ Save your final manuscript as "Master Document." From here on out, you will have multiple versions of the final book (as an eBook, print interior, etc.), but this will be the master document you refer back to.

eBook Interior

- ☐ If using eBook formatting software:
  - ○ Copy your manuscript into the software (if you did not compose in this software).
  - ○ Select design from pre-set options.
  - ○ Add headers and section titles.
  - ○ Review output.
  - ○ Save the eBook file as an ePub.
- ☐ If using MS Word:
  - ○ Review all formatting (headers, text, indentations).
  - ○ Save as a 1997-2003 .doc (NOT .DOCX).

> For eBooks, some platforms will allow you to upload a Microsoft Word document that has been formatted and will automatically generate the ePub or Mobi files. You can download that and upload it to the platforms that require ePub files.

Print Interior

- ☐ Create a new file in your print formatting software.
- ☐ Input the trim size, bleed, gutter, and trim based on your platform requirements.
- ☐ Input the text. (**NOTE**: some software will allow you to convert the eBook directly to print, some will not.)
- ☐ Review output.
- ☐ Save the print file as a PDF.

Each self-publishing platform has a file creation guide that will tell you in "design speak" the file type, color settings, bleed, trim, and other details for your print-ready file. Some will have a print interior template you can use. Some do not.

FINAL FILES SAVED LIST:

- ☐ ePub
- ☐ Mobi
- ☐ Print Interior PDF

Hiring a Formatter

That last page may look deceptively simple, but there are times when formatting can make you want to pull out your hair. That very first section required you to learn new software. How do you do with that usually? Keep in mind that you are the writer. You don't have to be a design expert too. If you have elected to hire a formatter out the gate or have recently realized that you have a fiery hatred for your computer because your attempts at formatting are not working, then here are the steps you will need to follow to hire a formatter.

Where to find an excellent formatter: You should use one or all of these options to find different formatters or formatting services to work with. Keep in mind that longer lists are harder to whittle down. Right now, we are looking at making a list of potential formatters. We will eliminate some options next.

- ❏ Pick out your favorite two or three books. Check the copyright page to confirm who formatted it. Search for their name online and jot down their contact information.
- ❏ Search for Book Formatting on Fiverr. Check the reviews and only add designers to your list whose style you like.
- ❏ Search for Book Formatting on Reedsy. Check the reviews and only add designers to your list whose style you like.
- ❏ Look at pricing for the different packages from Formatted Books. (They did the formatting for this book.)
- ❏ Ask other indie authors for recommendations.

VETTING POTENTIAL FORMATTERS

It is essential to ask questions at this stage. You will be able to whittle down your list quickly as you find out who is in and out of your price range, who has the experience to help, and who communicates with you. A few critical items to consider:

- What is included in the price? Are you just getting an ePub file? If you need other formats, what will that cost? Refer back to Page 50 to your list of formats. How many rounds will this include? Will you have access to print master files if you need to make a tiny typo change? If not, what will they charge for minor edits?

- Do they have experience with self-published books or traditionally published books? The formatter will know book design, but if they have only worked on traditionally published books, they will likely charge more and need you to provide the file creation guides and templates from your platforms.

- How do they communicate? What questions are they asking you? Do you think you will mesh well?

You will find a chart comparing your formatting options on the following pages. I have already input Formatted Books. I have worked with them as well as individual designers. Formatted Books should be part of your mix when considering who to work with. Maybe you elect to go with someone else, but keep them in the mix to start.

Comparing Formatting Options

Formatter	Contact Info	Quoted Price	Experience with Self-Published Books?	What is included in the project? (Compare against what you need)	Number of Design Rounds	Estimated Timeline for Final Files
Formatted Books	https://formattedbooks.com/?ref=31		YES	☐ ePub File ☐ Mobi File ☐ Print Interior File		
				☐ ePub File ☐ Mobi File ☐ Print Interior File		
				☐ ePub File ☐ Mobi File ☐ Print Interior File		

Formatter	Contact Info	Quoted Price	Experience with Self-Published Books?	What is included in the project? (Compare against what you need)	Number of Design Rounds	Estimated Timeline for Final Files
				☐ ePub File ☐ Mobi File ☐ Print Interior File		
				☐ ePub File ☐ Mobi File ☐ Print Interior File		
				☐ ePub File ☐ Mobi File ☐ Print Interior File		

Formatter	Contact Info	Quoted Price	Experience with Self-Published Books?	What is included in the project? (Compare against what you need)	Number of Design Rounds	Estimated Timeline for Final Files
				☐ ePub File ☐ Mobi File ☐ Print Interior File		
				☐ ePub File ☐ Mobi File ☐ Print Interior File		
				☐ ePub File ☐ Mobi File ☐ Print Interior File		

Professional Formatter Checklist

Now that you have decided which formatter or formatting service to use, this is the checklist to follow to ensure your book files are completed.

Refer back to Page 50 to confirm which formats you will need. Cross out any formats from the list below that you will NOT be using.

Research/Hiring

- ☐ Research potential formatters (Pages 215-217).
- ☐ Whittle down the list to the top two or three.
- ☐ Select your top formatter.
- ☐ Pay for services.
- ☐ Provide design brief. (Description of your book, books you want to compare to, desired categories, specific interior elements you want to see.)
- ☐ Provide the final manuscript file and any interior images.

> Some formatters will ask for the entire fee upfront. Others will do a down payment/ final payment set-up. Typically formatting services ask for the entire payment upfront. If you are working with an individual designer, you may be able to make multiple payments.

Revisions and Feedback

- ☐ Review the initial formatting concept design and your book elements:
  - ○ Italics match
  - ○ Bold match
  - ○ Underline match
  - ○ Indented passages
  - ○ Call out boxes
  - ○ Images or graphs
- ☐ Get feedback. (This can be your support team or other authors.)
- ☐ Provide feedback to the formatter.
- ☐ Review the next round. *CONFIRM YOU ARE NOT GOING OVER ON DESIGN ROUNDS*

> Designers have all gone through rigorous training and critiques. If you don't like the first concepts, be specific. What do you not like? What did you expect but not see? They are designers, not mind-readers.

Print File

- ☐ Lock in the final print interior file.
- ☐ Save the print interior file.

eBook File

- ☐ Review converted eBook file(s) on your eReading device or an emulator. You can use previewer apps on your desktop, like Kindle Previewer and Adobe Digital Editions. Or you can just email the file to yourself, download it on your smartphone, and open it up on your Kindle, OverDrive, Libby, or another preferred eReader app.
- ☐ Provide feedback on any eBook conversion errors.
- ☐ Lock in the final eBook file.
- ☐ Save the ePub and Mobi files.

Mobi files have only been used for Amazon Kindle and are being phased out. However, it is helpful to have both ePub and Mobi versions of your book during the transition.

Design Extras *IF this is part of your formatting contract*

- ☐ Save working files for the design.

FINAL FILES SAVED LIST:

- ☐ ePub
- ☐ Mobi
- ☐ Print Interior PDF

Children's Book List

If you are planning to write and self-publish a children's book, then the design is the most significant element of your book. Ideally, you want to work with someone who can do BOTH the illustration design AND formatting. Otherwise, you will have to hire a designer to create the images and have them work closely with your formatter so that the text on the page fits in with the images designed. It is possible to do, but more work (and cost) for everyone involved.

Let's start with some of the basics:

Age Range: _____

Words Per Page: _____

# of Pages Planned: _____

First, plan the amount of text on each page. Don't forget to include a title page, copyright page, dedication, and any end instructions for parents/educators. Then you will calculate your total number of pages needed. This will need to be an **even** number.

Style of design:

- ☐ Hand drawn
- ☐ Digital paint/animation
- ☐ Digital paper photos

Follow my interview series with children's book author Rob Phelan as he worked through every step of self-publishing his book and how he launched a successful Kickstarter campaign to fund it.

"Children's Book" is a wide age range from babies up through primary school. The complexity of the story, the number of words on a page, and the images will all vary.

Knowing the style you like will help you select an illustrator to work with. **Create a Pinterest board of styles and books you like.**

Next, you need to figure out what will be illustrated. You may want to work with a designer as a collaborator, or you may have a precise idea of what you want each page to look like. Start to write out these notes and determine which type of image you need: spot, full, or spread.

Design count:

_____ Spot illustrations

_____ Full-page illustrations

_____ Two-page spread
    illustrations

Spot **Full** **Spread**

Illustrator priorities: (select all the elements you want in your illustrator that apply)

- ❐ Experience with self-publishing
- ❐ Competitive price
- ❐ Print formatting
- ❐ Ebook formatting
- ❐ Cover design

Author priorities: (select all the elements that matter the most to you and that you will communicate to potential illustrators who apply)

- ❐ Speed to market
- ❐ Communication
- ❐ Collaboration

Do you have any plans to create related content to the children's book (e.g., stuffed animals, coloring books, stickers)?
    ❐ Yes   ❐ No

Communicate this with the designer so it can be part of the contract.

You will find a chart comparing your design options on the following pages I have already input Formatted Books and 1000StoryBooks. I have worked with both of these services as well as individual designers. These services should be part of your mix when considering who to work with. Maybe you elect to go with someone else, but keep them in the mix to start.

IMPORTANT NOTE

None of the print-on-demand self-publishing platforms offer the ability to print board books. If you want to create a board book or use a heavy cardstock for your book you will need to do a digital or offset print run and sell the book via Amazon Seller Central or your own website.

Comparing Design Options

Designer	Contact Info	Quoted Price	Experience with Self-Published Books?	What is included in the project? (Compare against what you need)	Number of Design Rounds	Estimated Timeline for Final Files
Formatted Books	https://formattedbooks.com/?ref=31		YES	☐ Interior illustrations ☐ Cover design ☐ eBook formatting ☐ Print book formatting ☐ Additional elements for promoting book		
1000Story Books	https://1000storybooks.com/		YES	☐ Interior illustrations ☐ Cover design ☐ eBook formatting ☐ Print book formatting ☐ Additional elements for promoting book		
				☐ Interior illustrations ☐ Cover design ☐ eBook formatting ☐ Print book formatting ☐ Additional elements for promoting book		

Designer	Contact Info	Quoted Price	Experience with Self-Published Books?	What is included in the project? (Compare against what you need)	Number of Design Rounds	Estimated Timeline for Final Files
				☐ Interior illustrations ☐ Cover design ☐ eBook formatting ☐ Print book formatting ☐ Additional elements for promoting book		
				☐ Interior illustrations ☐ Cover design ☐ eBook formatting ☐ Print book formatting ☐ Additional elements for promoting book		
				☐ Interior illustrations ☐ Cover design ☐ eBook formatting ☐ Print book formatting ☐ Additional elements for promoting book		

Designer	Contact Info	Quoted Price	Experience with Self-Published Books?	What is included in the project? (Compare against what you need)	Number of Design Rounds	Estimated Timeline for Final Files
				☐ Interior illustrations ☐ Cover design ☐ eBook formatting ☐ Print book formatting ☐ Additional elements for promoting book		
				☐ Interior illustrations ☐ Cover design ☐ eBook formatting ☐ Print book formatting ☐ Additional elements for promoting book		
				☐ Interior illustrations ☐ Cover design ☐ eBook formatting ☐ Print book formatting ☐ Additional elements for promoting book		

Professional Children's Book Designer Checklist

Now that you have decided which illustrator to use, this is the checklist to follow to ensure your book files are completed.

Refer back to Page 50 to confirm which formats you will need. Cross out any formats from the list below that you will NOT be using.

Research/Hiring

☐ Research potential illustrators or designers (Pages 222-224).

☐ Whittle down the list to the top two or three.

☐ Select your top illustrator.

☐ Pay for services.

☐ Provide design brief. (Description of your book, books you want to compare to, desired categories, specific interior elements you want to see, character descriptions, setting descriptions.)

☐ Provide the final manuscript file.

Some illustrators will ask for the entire fee upfront. Others will do a down payment/ final payment set-up. Typically design services ask for the entire payment upfront. If you are working with an individual designer, you may be able to make multiple payments.

Character Development

☐ Provide specific descriptions of each character to the illustrator.

☐ Review and provide feedback to the designer on each character sketch.

☐ Confirm locations in this phase. If you have a setting used on multiple pages, hash out the details now.

☐ Lock in character sketches and locations.

Designers have all gone through rigorous training and critiques. If you don't like the first concepts, be specific. What do you not like? What did you expect but not see? They are designers, not mind-readers.

Sketches

☐ Each page is sketched in black and white.

☐ Confirm all pages are provided. Make sure there is enough space for text on the appropriate pages.

The transition from the sketching (black-and-white) to the color phase is critical. Whether the illustrations are done by hand or digitally, it is more work (and money) to revise the base images once the color is applied.

- ☐ Review and provide feedback.
- ☐ Lock in black and white sketches.

Color Added

- ☐ Each page has color added.
- ☐ Confirm all pages are provided.
- ☐ Review and provide feedback.
- ☐ Lock in full-color images.

Final Files

- ☐ Confirm correct text is on each page.
- ☐ Review all pages.
- ☐ Lock in final formatting.

Print File

- ☐ Lock in the final print interior file.
- ☐ Save the print interior file.

Mobi files have only been used for Amazon Kindle and are being phased out. However, it is helpful to have both ePub and Mobi versions of your book during the transition.

eBook File

- ☐ Review converted eBook file on your eReading device or an emulator.
- ☐ Provide feedback on any eBook conversion errors.
- ☐ Lock in the final eBook file.
- ☐ Save ePub and Mobi files.

Design Extras *IF this is part of your formatting contract*

- ☐ Save working files for the design

FINAL FILES SAVED LIST:

- ☐ ePub
- ☐ Mobi
- ☐ Print Interior
- ☐ eBook Cover
- ☐ Paperback Cover

- ☐ Hardcover Files
- ☐ Audiobook Cover
- ☐ Additional images to promote the book/characters

Final Proofread

Now that you have all your files, it is time to read your book one last time. You are looking for any final errors or typos. (Remember, your formatter can only work with what you give them. If you have a typo in your manuscript, it will be there in your final files unless you say something.)

A tip for this final read is to go through the book backward.

Yes.

Read each sentence backward. It stops the flow of your brain and means you are looking at each sentence. Instead of getting into a flow and missing something, you are more likely to catch any lingering issues.

SECTION END:

After working through all the checklists in this section you should have the following:

- ☐ eBook cover (JPEG)
- ☐ eBook files (ePub, Mobi, PDF)
- ☐ Paperback cover (PDF)
- ☐ Paperback interior files (PDF)
- ☐ Hardcover case (PDF)
- ☐ Hardcover jacket (PDF)
- ☐ Hardcover interior files (PDF)
- ☐ Audiobook cover (PNG)
- ☐ Audiobook files (Refer back to Page 153 where we reviewed how to hire out or self-narrate.)

PRE-ORDER LAUNCH AND LAUNCH PLANNING

Now for the fun part! Planning WHEN you will tell the world that your book is available for order and when they will be able to read it. You have control here, but you also have to exercise some self-control. It is VERY tempting to have your finished files in hand and get the book out to everyone right now. But you didn't just spend X many months or years of your life on this book just to rush the release.

Here are some terms to keep in mind as you work through the following pages to plan out your book release:

PUBLICATION DATE – this is the "birthday" for your book. This is the date the book is published to the world and available to purchase immediately. For an eBook, the reader would be able to start reading within seconds; for a print book, the order will process and get to the reader as quickly as their shipping selection allows for.

PRE-ORDER – this is when the book is available on the major retailers for order, but the actual content is held until your publication date. This allows people to purchase now and get the book later. They have already paid, so on the book's "birthday," it will get to them as quickly as possible.

LAUNCH – this is a marketing term related to introducing and promoting a new product, in this case: your book.

After you work through this section, come back to fill in your final PUBLICATION DATE and PRE-ORDER ANNOUNCEMENT DATE (if you elect to have a pre-order). Be sure to also input these dates on your calendars from Pages 14-27.

PUBLICATION DATE: _____

PRE-ORDER ANNOUNCEMENT DATE: _____

> **PRO TIP**
>
> Don't make your publication date your birthday. I've seen too many authors scramble to get every detail in place because their birthday is around the corner. Details are missing, announcements are botched, and their birthday ends up becoming a reminder of a disappointing book launch. Give your book its own birthday. Hey, you get to celebrate twice.

Will You Do A Pre-Order For Your Book?

First, let's review WHY you would want to do a pre-order. This enables people to order your book now, but they won't get it until later. Won't they just want to read it right away? Maybe. Many readers are familiar with this strategy. It won't confuse most avid readers.

You can also explain in your pre-order marketing the benefit: each print pre-order sale will count on 12:01 am on your publication date. This can catapult your book to a higher ranking that day and increase visibility. For traditional publishers, this helps to ensure they print enough books. For us self-publishers using print-on-demand, the benefit is in the rankings.

But outside of that, the pre-order gives you a chance to remind people to order. Most people are (how do I put this politely?): Lazy. They NEED a reason to order your book and continual reminders. When you say, "Pre-Order my book by X date to help more readers discover it," that helps. When you say, "Pre-Order my book by X date for YZ promo offer," that really helps. You'll be marketing this book for the rest of your life, and you'll need new things to say about it all the time. Having a pre-order campaign gives you time to say many things about your book to drive sales.

But how long should this campaign be? Sometimes it is easier to work back from your ideal publication date to determine if you have the time to run a pre-order campaign. I usually recommend at least six to eight weeks for an effective pre-order campaign. If you are running up on your ideal publication date, you could do a very short pre-order or forgo it altogether.

IDEAL PUBLICATION DATE: _____

-8 WEEKS: _____ (Potential Pre-Order Launch)

TODAY'S DATE: _____

How much time do you have between now and this potential pre-order launch?

Is it enough time to get all your files formatted and the other technical set-up done?
❑ Yes   ❑ No

Why Should Someone Pre-Order Your Book?

We need to focus on why someone should take the time to pre-order your book. Your mom will pre-order it because she loves you. But why should anyone else? As an author, you can do as much or as little as you want to promote your pre-order. It will be more successful if you talk about it and promote it to your audience more. Having a reason to pre-order will give you more things to say.

Again, this is both an art and a science. If you have too many offers or interim deadlines, then it can be confusing for people. You want this to be simple and easy – make it as smooth as possible for someone to pre-order your book. The fewer hoops to jump through, the better.

Pre-Order Incentives

- ☐ Here are some options you can select to offer. You can also add some of your own.

- ☐ Pre-order price discount on the book

- ☐ Discount on series during the pre-order period

- ☐ Autographed copy (book plate) for pre-orders

- ☐ Exclusive Q&A

- ☐ Bonus chapter

- ☐ Deleted scene

- ☐ Alternate ending

- ☐ Book-related merchandise

- ☐ Thank you shout-out with their name and handle on social media

- ☐ _____

- ☐ _____

- ☐ _____

- ☐ _____

Pre-Order Important Dates

Format	Pre-Order Start Date	Publication Date	Pre-Order Length
eBook			
*Paperback**			
*Hardcover**			
*Audiobook***			

*Amazon KDP does not allow you to do a pre-order on print books. You can access this via a print aggregator like IngramSpark or LuLu.

**ACX only allows audiobook pre-orders with exclusive titles. You can set a pre-order on your audiobook via Findaway Voices.

SECTION END:

After working through all the checklists in this section, you should have the following:

- ☐ Will you do a pre-order for your book?
- ☐ If so, which formats?
- ☐ Will all formats launch at once?
- ☐ Why should someone pre-order your book?

UPLOADING ORDER OF OPERATION: UPLOAD, PUBLISH, AND DISTRIBUTE

HAVE A PLAN! Having your files can be so exciting, and you just want to click all the buttons. But guess what: you didn't just take almost a year to write and edit this thing to rush the upload process. This is you actually publishing the book!!

This is the easy part. You log in, fill in the information you've already assembled, upload your files, and hit publish. Despite the technical ease, this is the part that authors have the most trepidation about. This is the actual publication of the book! As long as you can easily fill out forms online, you should do fine in this section. You've already done the work to create each element. Now you're putting the pieces together.

In this section, there are four distinct upload order of operations checklists. **Pick ONE of them to use**:

- Order of Operations Option 1 – Amazon Only, No Pre-Order (Page 236)
- Order of Operations Option 2 – Amazon Only, Pre-Order (Page 238)
- Order of Operations Option 3 – Wide Distribution, No Pre-Order (Page 240)
- Order of Operations Option 4 – Wide Distribution, Pre-Order (Page 246)

    These are ordered from the least detailed checklist to the most complex.

After those checklists, you will find additional resources (Page 252) that apply regardless of your strategy:

- Ordering author copies of your book to proof and promote.
- Celebrating this huge milestone.

Before you upload, make sure to have the following in front of you:

- ❏ The Order of Operations Checklist for your strategy
- ❏ Your saved book and cover files
- ❏ Your Title
- ❏ Your ISBNs (Page 164)
- ❏ Your Book Description (Page 182)
- ❏ Your Categories (Page 174-175)
- ❏ Your Keywords (Page 176)
- ❏ Your Pricing Plan (Page 76)
- ❏ Your Wholesale Discount and Returnability Plan (Page 78)

PRO TIP

Have a document open on your computer with the title, description, keywords, categories, and ISBNs so you can easily copy and paste. This way, you can avoid transposing any letters or numbers.

I have upload tutorials for most major platforms on my YouTube channel. You can follow along with my tutorials to make the process easier. I will update them periodically as the different services change their websites.

Order of Operations Option 1

Strategy: Amazon Only, No Pre-Order

⧗ When To Tackle

-3 Days before Publication Date: _____

Amazon KDP states that it can take up to 72 hours to review and approve your book. That doesn't account for any errors you may have to correct. Don't wait until your publication date to upload.

Now is the time to upload. Log in to your Amazon KDP Account and get started:

- ☐ eBook upload
  - ○ eBook details
  - ○ eBook content – ALWAYS GO THROUGH EVERY PAGE OF THE PREVIEW
  - ○ eBook pricing
  - ○ Hit "Publish"
  - ○ Kindle Select Expiration Date (if applicable): _____ (add to your calendar)
- ☐ Paperback upload
  - ○ Add paperback to your eBook: You can add the paperback separately and link later, but it will take longer for everything to show up on one page. Also, by doing this, you don't have to enter the basic details again (title, description, keywords, etc.).
  - ○ Paperback content – ALWAYS GO THROUGH EVERY PAGE OF THE PREVIEW
  - ○ Paperback pricing
  - ○ Hit "Publish"
- ☐ Hardcover upload
  - ○ Add hardcover to your eBook: You can add the hardcover separately and link later, but it will take longer for everything to show up on one page. Also, by doing this, you don't have to enter the basic details again (title, description, keywords, etc.).
  - ○ Hardcover content – ALWAYS GO THROUGH EVERY PAGE OF THE PREVIEW
  - ○ Hardcover pricing
  - ○ Hit "Publish"

Now that we have published on KDP and are waiting for Amazon to review and approve all of your books on that platform, we can work on the audiobook.

- ☐ Audiobook upload to ACX **(+24 hours from Amazon KDP eBook live on Kindle Store)**
  - ○ "Assert title" – find your eBook in the catalog and claim
  - ○ Complete metadata and audiobook details
  - ○ Upload audio files
  - ○ Upload cover file
  - ○ Submit to Quality Assurance

NOTE: ACX can take up to 30 days to complete their Quality Assurance review of your audiobook, so you may not have it available to promote at the same time as the eBook and print books. This is okay – you'll have more to say about the book later.

- ☐ Confirm all formats are showing up on the book page on Amazon.com. (Can a reader easily toggle between eBook, paperback, and hardcover to purchase the edition they want?)

 DO NOT POST OR PROMOTE ANYTHING UNTIL ALL YOUR LINKS ARE LIVE AND THE FORMATS ARE LINKED. Posting the link as soon as the eBook is live is super tempting, but patience will pay off. Wait for all the formats to show.

Order of Operations Option 2

Strategy: Amazon Only, Pre-Order

Because you can only set a pre-order for your eBook and audiobook on KDP and ACX*, we need to break up our uploading process. Remember, **THERE IS NO PRINT PRE-ORDER AVAILABLE VIA AMAZON KDP**. You cannot do a print pre-order if you have an Amazon Only Strategy.

First, we'll upload our digital formats, and then – closer to the publication date – we will need to upload the print books.

⧗ When To Tackle

-3 Days before Pre-Order Announcement Date: _____

Amazon KDP states that it can take up to 72 hours to review and approve your book. That doesn't account for any errors you may have to correct. Don't wait until your pre-order announcement date to upload.

Now is the time to upload. Log in to your Amazon KDP Account and get started:

- ☐ eBook upload
  - ○ eBook details
  - ○ eBook content – ALWAYS GO THROUGH EVERY PAGE OF THE PREVIEW
    - • **YOU WILL SELECT THE PUBLICATION DATE ON THIS PAGE**
  - ○ eBook pricing
  - ○ Hit "Pre-Order"
  - ○ Kindle Select Expiration Date:_____ (add to your calendar)
- ☐ Audiobook upload to ACX **(+24 hours from KDP eBook live on Kindle Store)**
  - ○ "Assert title" – find your eBook in the catalog and claim
  - ○ Complete metadata and audiobook details
  - ○ Upload audio files
  - ○ Upload cover file
  - ○ Submit to Quality Assurance

NOTE: ACX can take up to 30 days to complete their Quality Assurance review of your audiobook, so you may not have it available to promote at the same time as the eBook and print books. This is okay – you'll have more to say about the book later.

*If you select the "exclusive" ACX contract, you can set the publication date. If you elect "non-exclusive," you cannot select the publication date.

⌛ When To Tackle

-3 Days before Publication Date: _____

Because you cannot elect a print pre-order on Amazon KDP, you have to upload your print books closer to your publication date. Remember, Amazon says it can take up to 72 hours to review and approve your files. You will upload before your publication date so that everything is live and linked on the publication date:

- ❏ Paperback upload
  - ○ Add paperback to your eBook: You can add the paperback separately and link later, but it will take longer for everything to show up on one page. Also, by doing this, you don't have to enter the basic details again (title, description, keywords, etc.).
  - ○ Paperback content – ALWAYS GO THROUGH EVERY PAGE OF THE PREVIEW
  - ○ Paperback pricing
  - ○ Hit "Publish"
- ❏ Hardcover upload
  - ○ Add hardcover to your eBook: You can add the hardcover separately and link later, but it will take longer for everything to show up on one page. Also, by doing this, you don't have to enter the basic details again (title, description, keywords, etc.).
  - ○ Hardcover content – ALWAYS GO THROUGH EVERY PAGE OF THE PREVIEW
  - ○ Hardcover pricing
  - ○ Hit "Publish"

Publication Day:

- ❏ Confirm all formats are showing up on the book page on Amazon.com. (Can a reader easily toggle between eBook, paperback, and hardcover to purchase the edition they want?)

Because **you cannot set up a print pre-order on Amazon**, I usually DO NOT recommend using this strategy if you plan to have print formats for your book. If you want to go "Amazon Only," I recommend launching everything simultaneously (see Page 236). If you want a pre-order for all formats, use a wide distribution strategy to set the publication date for all formats (see Page 246).

Order of Operations Option 3

Strategy: Wide Distribution, No Pre-Order

As we move into the more detailed checklists and advanced strategies, I have included a master checklist. There are detailed sub-lists for each platform, but you can check off your progress on the master checklist as well:

Master Checklist by Platform:

- ☐ Amazon KDP
- ☐ ACX
- ☐ Google Play
- ☐ Barnes & Noble Press
- ☐ Kobo Writing Life
- ☐ Apple Books for Authors
- ☐ IngramSpark
- ☐ Draft2Digital/Smashwords
- ☐ LuLu
- ☐ Findaway Voices

> This is my recommended order of operations. Start with your direct platforms first, then upload to aggregators. You likely will not use all of these platforms, but keep this order in mind:
>
> **DIRECT FIRST, THEN AGGREGATORS**

⌛ When To Tackle

-7 Days before Publication Date: _____

Because each platform can take time to process your files, you want to give yourself more than enough time to ensure that your book is showing on as many retailers as possible before you announce your book is published.

We will work in order from our direct retailers down to our aggregators. If there is a direct retailer you elected not to work with, cross out that retail from your list.

We want to upload to our direct retailers first to know which retailers to "unselect" or decline distribution when uploading to aggregators. If you are only working with an aggregator for simplicity, skip to that section. If you plan to only work with direct platforms, don't upload to the aggregators on this list.

Amazon KDP and ACX

- ☐ eBook upload
  - ○ eBook details
  - ○ eBook content – ALWAYS GO THROUGH EVERY PAGE OF THE PREVIEW
  - ○ eBook pricing
  - ○ Hit "Publish"
- ☐ Paperback upload
  - ○ Add paperback to your eBook: You can add the paperback separately and link later, but it will take longer for everything to show up on one page. Also, by doing this, you don't have to enter the basic details again (title, description, keywords, etc.).
  - ○ Paperback content – ALWAYS GO THROUGH EVERY PAGE OF THE PREVIEW
  - ○ Paperback pricing – DO NOT SELECT EXTENDED DISTRIBUTION
  - ○ Hit "Publish"
- ☐ Hardcover upload
  - ○ Add hardcover to your eBook: You can add the hardcover separately and link later, but it will take longer for everything to show up on one page. Also, by doing this, you don't have to enter the basic details again (title, description, keywords, etc.).
  - ○ Hardcover content – ALWAYS GO THROUGH EVERY PAGE OF THE PREVIEW
  - ○ Hardcover pricing – DO NOT SELECT EXTENDED DISTRIBUTION
  - ○ Hit "Publish"

Now that we have published on KDP and are waiting for Amazon to review and approve all of your books on that platform, we can work on the audiobook.

- ☐ Audiobook upload to ACX **(+24 hours from KDP eBook live on Kindle Store)**
  - ○ "Assert title" – find your eBook in the catalog and claim
  - ○ Complete metadata and audiobook details
  - ○ Upload audio files
  - ○ Upload cover file
  - ○ Submit to Quality Assurance

NOTE: ACX can take up to 30 days to complete their Quality Assurance review of your audiobook, so you may not have it available to promote at the same time as the eBook and print books. This is okay – you'll have more to say about the book later.

Google Play

- ☐ eBook upload
  - ○ eBook details
  - ○ eBook content
  - ○ eBook pricing
  - ○ Hit "Publish"
- ☐ Auto-narrated audiobook upload
  - ○ Audiobook details
  - ○ Audiobook content – review converted eBook text to narration
  - ○ Audiobook pricing
  - ○ Hit "Publish"

Barnes & Noble Press

- ☐ eBook upload
  - ○ eBook details
  - ○ eBook content – ALWAYS GO THROUGH EVERY PAGE OF THE PREVIEW
  - ○ eBook pricing
  - ○ Hit "Publish"
- ☐ Paperback upload
  - ○ Add paperback to your eBook: You can add the paperback separately and link later, but it will take longer for everything to show up on one page. Also, by doing this, you don't have to enter the basic details again (title, description, keywords, etc.).
  - ○ Paperback content – ALWAYS GO THROUGH EVERY PAGE OF THE PREVIEW
  - ○ Paperback pricing
  - ○ Hit "Publish"
- ☐ Hardcover upload
  - ○ Add hardcover to your eBook: You can add the hardcover separately and link later, but it will take longer for everything to show up on one page. Also, by doing this, you don't have to enter the basic details again (title, description, keywords, etc.).
  - ○ Hardcover content – ALWAYS GO THROUGH EVERY PAGE OF THE PREVIEW
  - ○ Hardcover pricing
  - ○ Hit "Publish"

Kobo Writing Life

- ❑ eBook upload
  - ○ eBook details
  - ○ eBook content – ALWAYS GO THROUGH EVERY PAGE OF THE PREVIEW
  - ○ eBook pricing
  - ○ Hit "Publish"
- ❑ Audiobook upload
  - ○ Audiobook details
  - ○ Audiobook content
  - ○ Audiobook pricing
  - ○ Hit "Publish"

Apple Books for Authors

- ❑ eBook upload
  - ○ eBook details
  - ○ eBook content – ALWAYS GO THROUGH EVERY PAGE OF THE PREVIEW
  - ○ eBook pricing
  - ○ Hit "Publish"
- ❑ Audiobook upload
  - ○ Audiobook details
  - ○ Audiobook content
  - ○ Audiobook pricing
  - ○ Hit "Publish"

Next, we are going to upload to our selected aggregators. **Be sure to "unselect" distribution to the retailers you already have your book listed with directly.** If there is an aggregator you elected not to work with, cross that one out of your list. Ideally, you should only use **ONE** of these aggregators for eBooks and print and Findaway Voices for audiobooks.

IngramSpark

- [ ] eBook upload
  - eBook details
  - eBook pricing
  - eBook content
  - Hit "Publish"
- [ ] Paperback upload
  - Paperback details
  - Paperback pricing
  - Paperback content
  - Hit "Publish"
  - Review digital proof and approve for distribution
- [ ] Hardcover upload
  - Hardcover details
  - Hardcover pricing
  - Hardcover content
  - Hit "Publish"
  - Review digital proof and approve for distribution

Draft2Digital/Smashwords

- [ ] eBook upload
  - eBook details
  - eBook pricing
  - eBook content – ALWAYS GO THROUGH EVERY PAGE OF THE PREVIEW
  - Hit "Publish"
- [ ] Paperback upload
  - Paperback details
  - Paperback pricing
  - Paperback content – ALWAYS GO THROUGH EVERY PAGE OF THE PREVIEW
  - Hit "Publish"
  - Review digital proof and approve for distribution

LuLu

- [ ] eBook upload
  - eBook details
  - eBook pricing
  - eBook content – ALWAYS GO THROUGH EVERY PAGE OF THE PREVIEW
  - Hit "Publish"
- [ ] Paperback upload
  - Paperback details
  - Paperback pricing
  - Paperback content
  - Review digital proof and approve
  - Hit "Publish"
- [ ] Hardcover upload
  - Hardcover details
  - Hardcover pricing
  - Hardcover content – ALWAYS GO THROUGH EVERY PAGE OF THE PREVIEW
  - Review digital proof and approve for distribution
  - Hit "Publish"

Findaway Voices

- [ ] Audiobook upload
  - Audiobook details
  - Audiobook pricing
  - Audiobook content
  - Submit to Quality Assurance
- [ ] Confirm all formats are showing up on the book page on your retailers, (Can a reader easily toggle between eBook, paperback, and hardcover to purchase the edition they want?)

 DO NOT POST OR PROMOTE ANYTHING UNTIL ALL YOUR LINKS (OR A MAJORITY) ARE LIVE AND THE FORMATS ARE LINKED. Posting the link as soon as the eBook is live is super tempting, but patience will pay off. Wait for all the formats to show.

Order of Operations Option 4

Strategy: Wide Distribution, Pre-Order

This strategy is more complicated with additional dates and platforms. However, this strategy can give you the best chance for success, reaching audiences across multiple platforms, and providing a pre-order opportunity to help boost rankings and visibility. This strategy is the only way to have your print book available for pre-order on Amazon.com. This is the strategy that I use, but that's for me. If you want the easiest option, go back to Option 1.

As we move into the more detailed checklists and advanced strategies, I have included a master checklist. There are detailed sub-lists for each platform, but you can check off your progress on the master checklist as well:

Master Checklist by Platform:

- ❐ Amazon KDP
- ❐ ACX
- ❐ Google Play
- ❐ Barnes & Noble Press
- ❐ Kobo Writing Life
- ❐ Apple Books for Authors
- ❐ IngramSpark
- ❐ Draft2Digital/Smashwords
- ❐ LuLu
- ❐ Findaway Voices

> This is my recommended order of operations. Start with your direct platforms first, then upload to aggregators. You likely will not use all of these platforms, but keep this order in mind:
>
> **DIRECT FIRST, THEN AGGREGATORS**

 **When To Tackle**

-7 Days before Pre-Order Announcement Date: _____

Because each platform can take time to process your files, you want to give yourself more than enough time to ensure that your book is showing on as many retailers as possible before you announce your book is published.

We will work in order from our direct retailers down to our aggregators. If there is a direct retailer you elected not to work with, cross out that retailer from your list.

Amazon KDP and ACX

Now it is time to upload. Log in to your Amazon KDP Account and get started:

- ❑ eBook upload
  - ○ eBook details
  - ○ eBook content – ALWAYS GO THROUGH EVERY PAGE OF THE PREVIEW
    - • **YOU WILL SELECT THE PUBLICATION DATE ON THIS PAGE**
  - ○ eBook pricing
  - ○ Hit "Pre-Order"

Now that we have uploaded to KDP and are waiting for Amazon to review and approve your book on that platform, we can work on the audiobook.

- ❑ Audiobook upload to ACX **(+24 hours from KDP eBook live on Kindle Store)**
  - ○ "Assert title" – find your eBook in the catalog and claim
  - ○ Complete metadata and audiobook details
  - ○ Upload audio files
  - ○ Upload cover file
  - ○ Submit to Quality Assurance

Your aggregator will distribute your print book to Amazon.com for your print pre-order. However, you will upload your print books to Amazon KDP to be sold directly on Amazon.com after publication. This is discussed on PAGE 251 at the end of this checklist.

NOTE: ACX can take up to 30 days to complete their Quality Assurance review of your audiobook, so you may not have it available to promote at the same time as the eBook and print books. This is okay – you'll have more to say about the book later.

*If you select the "exclusive" ACX contract, you can set the publication date. If you elect "non-exclusive," you cannot select the publication date.

Google Play

- ❑ eBook upload
  - ○ eBook details
  - ○ eBook content
  - ○ eBook pricing
  - ○ Hit "Pre-Order"
- ❑ Auto-narrated audiobook upload
  - ○ Audiobook details
  - ○ Audiobook content – review converted eBook text to narration

- o   Audiobook pricing
- o   Hit "Pre-Order"

Barnes & Noble Press

- ☐ eBook upload
  - o   eBook details
  - o   eBook content – ALWAYS GO THROUGH EVERY PAGE OF THE PREVIEW
  - o   eBook pricing
  - o   Hit "Pre-Order"
- ☐ Paperback upload
  - o   Add paperback to your eBook: You can add the paperback separately and link later, but it will take longer for everything to show up on one page. Also, by doing this, you don't have to enter the basic details again (title, description, keywords, etc.).
  - o   Paperback content – ALWAYS GO THROUGH EVERY PAGE OF THE PREVIEW
  - o   Paperback pricing
  - o   Hit "Pre-Order"
- ☐ Hardcover upload
  - o   Add hardcover to your eBook: You can add the hardcover separately and link later, but it will take longer for everything to show up on one page. Also, by doing this, you don't have to enter the basic details again (title, description, keywords, etc.).
  - o   Hardcover content – ALWAYS GO THROUGH EVERY PAGE OF THE PREVIEW
  - o   Hardcover pricing
  - o   Hit "Pre-Order"

Kobo Writing Life

- ☐ eBook upload
  - o   eBook details
  - o   eBook content – ALWAYS GO THROUGH EVERY PAGE OF THE PREVIEW
  - o   eBook pricing
  - o   Hit "Pre-Order"
- ☐ Audiobook upload
  - o   Audiobook details
  - o   Audiobook content
  - o   Audiobook pricing
  - o   Hit "Pre-Order"

Apple Books for Authors

- ☐ eBook upload
  - ○ eBook details
  - ○ eBook content – ALWAYS GO THROUGH EVERY PAGE OF THE PREVIEW
  - ○ eBook pricing
  - ○ Hit "Pre-Order"
- ☐ Audiobook upload
  - ○ Audiobook details
  - ○ Audiobook content
  - ○ Audiobook pricing
  - ○ Hit "Pre-Order"

Next, we are going to upload to our selected aggregators. **Be sure to "unselect" distribution to the retailers you already have your book listed with directly.** If there is an aggregator you elected not to work with, cross out that retailer from your list. Ideally, you should only use **ONE** of these aggregators for eBooks and print and Findaway Voices for audiobooks.

IngramSpark

On the pricing page, you will select both the publication and street date as your planned **publication date** to set the pre-order.

- ☐ eBook upload
  - ○ eBook details
  - ○ eBook pricing
  - ○ eBook content
  - ○ Hit "Publish"
- ☐ Paperback upload
  - ○ Paperback details
  - ○ Paperback pricing
  - ○ Paperback content
  - ○ Hit "Publish"
  - ○ Review digital proof and approve for distribution
- ☐ Hardcover upload
  - ○ Hardcover details
  - ○ Hardcover pricing
  - ○ Hardcover content
  - ○ Hit "Publish"
  - ○ Review digital proof and approve for distribution

Draft2Digital/Smashwords

- ☐ eBook upload
  - ○ eBook details
  - ○ eBook pricing
  - ○ eBook content – ALWAYS GO THROUGH EVERY PAGE OF THE PREVIEW
  - ○ Hit "Pre-Order"
- ☐ Paperback upload
  - ○ Paperback details
  - ○ Paperback pricing
  - ○ Paperback content – ALWAYS GO THROUGH EVERY PAGE OF THE PREVIEW
  - ○ Hit "Pre-Order"
  - ○ Review digital proof and approve for distribution

LuLu

- ☐ eBook upload
  - ○ eBook details
  - ○ eBook pricing
  - ○ eBook content – ALWAYS GO THROUGH EVERY PAGE OF THE PREVIEW
  - ○ Hit "Publish"
- ☐ Paperback upload
  - ○ Paperback details
  - ○ Paperback pricing
  - ○ Paperback content – ALWAYS GO THROUGH EVERY PAGE OF THE PREVIEW
  - ○ Review digital proof and approve
  - ○ Hit "Pre-Order"
- ☐ Hardcover upload
  - ○ Hardcover details
  - ○ Hardcover pricing
  - ○ Hardcover content – ALWAYS GO THROUGH EVERY PAGE OF THE PREVIEW
  - ○ Review digital proof and approve for distribution
  - ○ Hit "Pre-Order"

Findaway Voices

- ☐ Audiobook upload
  - ○ Audiobook details
  - ○ Audiobook pricing

- o   Audiobook content
- o   Hit "Publish"

Pre-Order Announcement Day:

☐   Confirm all formats are showing up on the book page on your retailers. (Can a reader easily toggle between eBook, paperback, and hardcover to purchase the edition they want?)

 DO NOT POST ANYTHING UNTIL ALL YOUR LINKS ARE LIVE AND THE FORMATS ARE LINKED. Posting the link as soon as the eBook is live is super tempting, but patience will pay off. Wait for all the formats and retailers to show.

⏳ When To Tackle

+1 Days after Publication Date: _____

Because you cannot elect a print pre-order on Amazon KDP, you have to upload your print books after your pre-order has concluded. Your aggregator was able to get your books listed on Amazon.com for pre-order, but now we want to maximize royalties:

☐   Paperback upload
- o   Add paperback to your eBook: You can add the paperback separately and link later, but it will take longer for everything to show up on one page. Also, by doing this, you don't have to enter the basic details again (title, description, keywords, etc.).
- o   Paperback content – ALWAYS GO THROUGH EVERY PAGE OF THE PREVIEW
- o   Paperback pricing – DO NOT SELECT EXTENDED DISTRIBUTION
- o   Hit "Publish"
☐   Hardcover upload
- o   Add hardcover to your eBook: You can add the hardcover separately and link later, but it will take longer for everything to show up on one page. Also, by doing this, you don't have to enter the basic details again (title, description, keywords, etc.).
- o   Hardcover content – ALWAYS GO THROUGH EVERY PAGE OF THE PREVIEW
- o   Hardcover pricing – DO NOT SELECT EXTENDED DISTRIBUTION
- o   Hit "Publish"

Author Copies Ordered

For those who have elected to add print books to their plan, you will need (and probably want) to get a copy in your hands as soon as possible. You have a couple of options here:

1. Proof copy
2. Author copy

A **proof copy** is typically ordered before your editing is completed and used as a final proofread. The expectation is that you would mark this up and address any final edits and tweaks BEFORE the book publication. With Amazon KDP, when you order a proof copy, there is a gray band around the book that reads "PROOF COPY NOT FOR RESALE." With IngramSpark, your proof copy will not have this.

An **author copy** looks precisely like a reader copy. There are no markings on the book. You order the books at cost and can use them for marketing and promotions, to hand out, or to keep.

You usually want to have several author copies to hand out to family and friends, to keep on your bookshelf, or to have on hand for promotions.

As you plan your order of author copies, use this checklist to ensure you have everything:

Order Planning

Date Books Ordered: _____

Expected Shipping Date: _____

# of Books in Order: _____

Cost of the Order: $ _____ (include tax, shipping, and handling fees)

*Add to your budget on Page 35

Cost per book: $ _____

Book Delivery Day:

 DO NOT OPEN THE BOX UNTIL YOU ARE READY TO FILM/
PHOTOGRAPH THIS MOMENT.

- ❏ Photograph/film unboxing to post later.
- ❏ Check the order to confirm you received the correct number of books.
- ❏ Look at each book for potential defects. Photograph any issues. (Expect SOME variation. You're looking for blatant issues with pages missing or falling out, boot prints on the book, etc.)
- ❏ Take promotional photos of your books on your bookshelf, desk, etc.

Celebration Planning

You just published your book! Take that in. You. Published. Your. Book! This is a huge moment. Even if you still have the entire pre-order to market the book or if it is live right now, uploading and hitting "publish" is a big moment. But often, it doesn't feel that way because we have all this marketing to do. Be sure to take time to celebrate. And the best way to make sure you celebrate is to have a plan in place.

How will I celebrate this milestone?

_____

_____

_____

_____

_____

_____

Who will I celebrate with?

_____

_____

_____

_____

_____

Special food/drinks:

_____

_____

_____

_____

_____

MARKETING

TECH-SAVVY

how hard is this step?

hard - requires tech skills
& patience!

easy - most every author
can tackle on their own

START MARKETING ON DAY 1

Even though this section is at the back of this workbook, you need to start marketing your book on Day 1. The day you start writing it, you need to start promoting it. This isn't to say, "buy my book. Oops, I have to write it." But start talking about the book, your process, your ideas, and your roadblocks. You need to bring people along with your journey so that when you have a finished book for them to check out, they feel that they have been rooting for you all along and are now excited to read this book finally.

To make it a bit easier, I've written down some ideas for what you can say/post throughout the different phases:

Writing

- ❏ Writing set up (desk, coffee, tea, etc.)
- ❏ Current challenges in your work in progress
- ❏ Daily word count goal
- ❏ Reading these books as research…
- ❏ Annoying neighbor sounds during your writing

Editing

- ❏ Revision progress
- ❏ Revision anxiety
- ❏ Draft completion
- ❏ "Just sent it off to the editors. Now what?"
- ❏ "Just got my manuscript back *hyperventilates into a bag*"
- ❏ Another day, another cup of coffee, another round of edits…

Set-Up

- ❏ Just got my first cover concepts. What do you think?
- ❏ Just picked my cover – it is beautiful! Stay tuned for the reveal on MM/DD
- ❏ Saw the interior for my book – it finally looks like a real book. It's happening!!

Publication

- ☐ Just hit "publish" on KDP... stay tuned for a link to pre-order soon!
- ☐ Banging my head against the keyboard. The book is so close to going live. So close!
- ☐ Big announcement next week about my book and some special pre-order offers.

Ongoing

- ☐ Now available on XYZ Retailer, check out [TITLE].
- ☐ So grateful for each review. Check out this amazing Five-Star Review...
- ☐ The perfect read for this [SEASON]...

AUTHOR WEBSITE

Many experts, myself included, advocate that every author has a website. This is your place on the internet. You own your website no matter what happens to your retailers or social media profiles.

Having your own website does not have to be expensive, complex, or fancy. Most hosting platforms have easy-to-use WYSIWYG (what you see is what you get) builders that look and function much like a regular word processor. You can drag and drop images. In general, the more simple the design, the better. It doesn't need to be crazy. And you can always upgrade and improve over time. If you feel really out of your depth, you can always hire someone to help.

TECH-SAVVY
how hard is this step?

hard – requires tech skills & patience!

easy – most every author can tackle on their own

⧗ When To Tackle

Try to set this up BEFORE you finalize the cover and send the book for formatting. This way, you can include any necessary links in the body of the book, back matter, or on the back cover.

Here is a super basic breakdown of how to start your website and what to add:

- ☐ Select a hosting platform: WordPress, Wix, Squarespace, etc.
- ☐ Acquire a domain name that works for your author brand. This should be a ".com," ".co," or another common domain, not one that includes the ".wordpress," ".wix," or ".squarespace" platform in the URL.
- ☐ Create a website. Plan your content ahead of time and have it reviewed for spelling and grammar.
- ☐ Add book to your website – description, links to purchase, any advanced reviews or praise. You can update this page as needed.
- ☐ Add your author biography. Who are you?
- ☐ Add a link to subscribe. (See Page 260)
- ☐ Over time, add a media kit, links to any press or interviews, book club guides, etc.
- ☐ Create any needed landing pages for pre-orders or ARC sign-ups.
- ☐ **PUBLICATION DAY**: Turn over links from "pre-order" to "buy now."

URL TIPS

- You can get a URL that matches your book title, but then with each new book, you will need to acquire a new URL and work to point traffic to that website.
- You can get a URL with your author's name and use that for all your books.
- It should be easy to spell and remember when you tell someone on a podcast or another interview.

These are the basics. You can learn to optimize and continue to redesign your website over time. For your launch, the minimum will suffice, but you may quickly realize you want to add more or offer new content to your readers and fans.

For any images, graphs, charts, or bibliographic references in your book, you can provide a link to a page on your website with expanded images or links to references. This can be especially helpful if you have exercises or worksheets to complete. It can also help listeners access content they miss out on in the audiobook.

EMAIL MARKETING

Your newsletter list is incredibly valuable. No matter how clever your social media posts are, you can't control the algorithm or other things popping up in reader's feeds on a given day. But with the ability to email a reader, you can directly remind them to order and review your book. You can also build excitement for your upcoming book and have a better relationship with these subscribers by offering them behind-the-scenes information and special perks for joining your list.

Having an email list and sending out a newsletter is a best practice. But it takes time, and if you put it on the back burner, so be it. But I did that for years. My day job involved email marketing. The last thing I wanted to do at home was more newsletter copy. I wanted to write my books. Well, not having a newsletter was a big mistake.

TECH-SAVVY

how hard is this step?

hard – requires tech skills & patience!

easy – most every author can tackle on their own

⧗ When To Tackle

Try to set this up BEFORE you finalize the cover and send the book for formatting. This way, you can include any necessary reader magnets in the body of the book, back matter, or on the back cover.

For the sake of getting your list started, here are the basics:

- ☐ Select an email service provider: MailChimp, ActiveCampaign, ConvertKit, etc.
- ☐ Set up an email subscription form and automated email response to subscribers.
- ☐ Add a link to subscribe to your website.
- ☐ Create a reader magnet.
- ☐ Post your reader magnet to your social media accounts.
- ☐ **PRE-ORDER LAUNCH**
  - ○ Invite your subscriber list to sign up as Advance Review Copy (ARC) Readers (Page 269)
  - ○ Detail pre-order benefits (Page 231)
- ☐ Reminder 1 – depending on the length of your pre-order, you may not send more than one reminder. Remember that you should have a balance on how often you email.
- ☐ Reminder 2
- ☐ Reminder 3
- ☐ **PUBLICATION DAY**: Send a final email to your list letting them know the book is live, thanking them for your support, and reminding them to share the news and leave a review.

READERS MAGNETS

Why should someone subscribe to your list? What value can you give them? Our inboxes are flooded with emails we don't have time to read. How can you get the reader interested in what you have to say?

Some options:

- Early access to your forthcoming book.
- Bonus chapters.
- Character side-stories.
- Alternative endings.
- Deleted scenes.
- Worksheets and activities that complement your topic.
- Discounts on your books to subscribers.

I used to work in email marketing for a major company, so I did a masterclass video on email marketing for authors that you can reference.

SOCIAL MEDIA

In addition to promoting your book to your "owned" media (your website and email list), you will want to leverage social media. I know, it is a time suck. Feeds are either full or doom-and-gloom or adorable kittens. How can you compete with the kittens?!?

Here are my top tips:

- ❑ The key here is consistency. Be positive. Be creative. And show up to do more than just say, "buy my book!"
- ❑ Pick a platform you feel more comfortable with and stick with it.
- ❑ Claim your handle across social media so no one else can sit on it. Even if you only plan to post to one platform, ensure no one else can sit on it.
- ❑ Research hashtags to use to amplify your posts.
- ❑ Connect (genuinely connect) with other creators in your genre. Support their work and posts. Collaborate and cross-promote with them. It makes it easier for them to say yes to helping you once you have helped them. But be genuine. People can smell a fake offer of help a mile away.

I will not go over every nuance of these major social media platforms. The following pages have lists specific to your book launch. Use the prompts from Page 256 to build content on that platform outside the launch period.

TECH-SAVVY
how hard is this step?

hard – requires tech skills & patience!

easy – most every author can tackle on their own

⏳ When To Tackle

Claim your profiles and start sharing your writing experience on Day 1 if you can (see Page 256).

Facebook

- ☐ ***Claim your author profile page***
- ☐ ***Invite people to like it***
- ☐ Announce cover reveal (can be the same as the pre-order announcement)
- ☐ ARC sign-up post
- ☐ Announce pre-order
  - ○ Update Cover Image with pre-order details
- ☐ Reminder 1
- ☐ Reminder 2
- ☐ Reminder 3
- ☐ **PUBLICATION DAY** Post
  - ○ Update Cover Image with "Book on sale now!" (no longer pre-order)
- ☐ Facebook Ads
  - ○ Optional. Look at the price and reach

Twitter

- ☐ ***Claim your author Twitter handle or use personal* – *you decide***
- ☐ ***Follow other authors and writers***
- ☐ Look at trending hashtags relevant to your genre and topic
- ☐ Announce cover reveal (can be the same as the pre-order announcement)
- ☐ ARC sign-up post
- ☐ Announce pre-order
  - ○ Update Cover Image with pre-order details
- ☐ Reminder 1
- ☐ Reminder 2
- ☐ Reminder 3
- ☐ **PUBLICATION DAY** Post
  - ○ Update Cover Image with "Book on sale now!" (no longer pre-order)
- ☐ Twitter Ads
  - ○ Optional. Look at the price and reach

Instagram

- ☐ ***Claim your author Instagram handle or use personal – you decide***
- ☐ ***Follow other authors and writers***
- ☐ Look at trending hashtags relevant to your genre and topic
- ☐ Find bookstagram influencers in your genre who match your aesthetic and taste. Reach out about their process for picking the books they review. (See Page 279 for more planning)
- ☐ Announce cover reveal (can be the same as the pre-order announcement)
- ☐ ARC sign-up post
- ☐ Announce pre-order
  - ○ Update Bio pre-order details (pub date and book title) and link to pre-order/purchase
- ☐ Reminder 1
- ☐ Reminder 2
- ☐ Reminder 3
- ☐ **PUBLICATION DAY** Post
  - ○ Update Bio with on-sale details (no longer pre-order)
- ☐ Instagram Ads
  - ○ Optional. Look at the price and reach

TikTok

- ☐ ***Claim your author TikTok handle or use personal – you decide***
- ☐ ***Follow other authors and writers***
- ☐ Look at trending hashtags relevant to your genre and topic
- ☐ Find BookTok influencers in your genre who match your aesthetic and taste. Reach out about their process for picking the books they review. (See Page 279 for more planning)
- ☐ Announce cover reveal
- ☐ ARC sign-up post
- ☐ Announce pre-order
  - ○ Update Bio pre-order details (pub date and book title) and link to pre-order/purchase
- ☐ Reminder 1
- ☐ Reminder 2
- ☐ Reminder 3

- ☐ **PUBLICATION DAY** Post
  - ○ Update Bio Links to "order" (not pre-order anymore)
- ☐ TikTok Ad
  - ○ Optional. Look at the price and reach

YouTube

Do you have a channel?
If no, then skip to Page 266.
If yes, then do these items.

Building a following on YouTube takes time and is a long-term content marketing strategy. With everything else going on with your launch, this isn't the time to launch a channel unless you are already interested in doing so.

- ☐ Cover reveal video
- ☐ Find booktube influencers in your genre who match your aesthetic and taste. Reach out about their process for picking the books they review. (See Page 279 for more planning)
- ☐ Pre-Order announcement video
- ☐ ARC sign-up video and community post
- ☐ Pre-Order Exclusive Video (set to private, only send to those who pre-order if this is part of your incentives)
- ☐ Launch day thank you video or live reading (or both!)

LAUNCH MARKETING

Launch Marketing Starts with ARC Copies

Since we have focused on getting your book ready to publish, most of our marketing focus in this workbook will be on your launch. And the first thing you need to help with your launch is rave reviews. Those come from your early readers. This is your hype squad. These readers get early access to your book, so they can rave about it and tell the world how amazing it is. This group is known as ARC (Advance Review Copy) Readers. But first, we need to assemble this team.

⧗ When To Tackle

You can have people start to sign up for the ARC team as soon as you begin writing the book. But remember that you'll have to ask people to re-up their commitment once you have the files. I like to start asking once I have the final files to send out.

Build ARC Team

First, we need to know who this team is. Distinct from your Beta Readers (Page 141), this group will read the finished book. They agree to read the book by your launch date and leave an honest review when it launches. Therefore, you need to ASK people to join this team. You cannot assume that because someone subscribes to your email list, they are going to be an ARC reader. They may not have time to read the book before your launch. They could have missed that one email.

We also need to give them a reason to join your ARC team. Your friends and family will happily to sign up to help you out. They'll read and share all your social posts. But why should someone else? These benefits should be distinct from your pre-order incentives (Page 231).

Also, keep in mind that the completion rate may be low. Your best friend's mom promised she would read it and leave a rave review. When she finished the book, she texted, "couldn't put it down, read until dawn. AMAZING!!!" with extra emojis. But then, the review never materialized online. All that enthusiasm, but no one else will know she loved it. It happens. Be realistic and keep your expectations low. Then, if everyone leaves a review, you will be over-the-moon thrilled.

 BECAUSE YOU ARE ASKING YOUR ARC READERS TO READ AND LEAVE AN HONEST REVIEW, YOU CANNOT OFFER ANY FINANCIAL GIFT OR CONDITIONAL BENEFITS. AS IN, EVERY ARC READER GETS THE BENEFIT REGARDLESS OF WHETHER THEY LEAVE A REVIEW OR NOT!! OTHERWISE, YOUR BOOK MAY GET FLAGGED AND TAKEN DOWN.

ARC Team Incentives

- ❒ Here are some options you can select to offer. You can also add some of your own.
- ❒ Free copy of the book (Obvi!)
- ❒ Autographed copy (book plate)
- ❒ Exclusive Q&A
- ❒ Bonus chapter
- ❒ Deleted scene
- ❒ Alternate ending
- ❒ Book related merchandise
- ❒ Thank you shout-out with their name and handle on social media
- ❒ _____
- ❒ _____
- ❒ _____
- ❒ _____

Here is how you get people to sign on for your ARC team:

- ❑ Create a form for readers to sign up. Ask them to confirm the following:
  - ○ Email address to contact them with
  - ○ What format would they like (ePub, PDF, audiobook)
  - ○ Agree to read by **PUBLICATION DATE**
  - ○ Which retailers will they leave an honest review on
- ❑ Include the sign-up form in an email to your newsletter list.
- ❑ Post the sign-up form on your social media.
- ❑ Send book to those who sign-up.
- ❑ Reminder 1 – Send -**2 weeks before PUBLICATION DATE**
- ❑ Reminder 2 – **-1 Day before PUBLICATION DATE**
- ❑ Reminder 3 – **PUBLICATION DATE**
- ❑ Reminder 4 - **+7 Days after PUBLICATION DATE**

ARC TEAM EMAIL INVITE SCRIPT

"[TITLE] is almost here! The book will go on pre-order soon. As a subscriber, I want you to get the first chance to sign-up for my launch team.

Being on the launch team means you'll read or listen to the book before it launches (you'll get a FREE digital copy from me). When the book launches, you'll leave an honest review (good, bad, great, horrible) for the book and help amplify the release by sharing my social posts.

Writing and launching a book can be lonely; having a supportive launch team makes this more fun. Sign up for the launch team here: WWW.LINK.COM."

REMINDER EMAILS

Here are the basics you need to cover in each reminder email.

2 Weeks Prior

- Highlight any positive pre-order rankings or press for the book.
- Confirm receipt of book (if not already done).
- Launch date reminder.

1 Day Prior

- Highlight any positive pre-order rankings or press for the book.
- Thank you for being on ARC Team.
- Reminder to post their review tomorrow.

Publication Day

- Thank you!
- Launch date exciting details and news.
- "Please send reviews once posted so I can share on social media…"

+7 Days Post Publication

- Thank you!
- Launch date exciting details and news.
- "Please send reviews once posted so I can share on social media…"

ARC Team

Name	Contact Information	Book Sent? Yes/No	Confirm Receipt? Yes/No	Book Finished? Yes/No	Review Posted? Yes/No	Thank You Sent Yes/No

Name	Contact Information	Book Sent? Yes/No	Confirm Receipt? Yes/No	Book Finished? Yes/No	Review Posted? Yes/No	Thank You Sent Yes/No

LAUNCH MARKETING MESSAGES

Next, let's go over how you will market your book for launch. You only get one launch; this is your big moment to make a splash. (If you miss your launch, you can always do another big push later, but try to make the most of this special time frame.)

Your **launch period** is when you are promoting the book's release. If you aren't doing a pre-order, your launch period is the day you announce the book is for sale and the following weeks. If you will have a pre-order for your book, your launch period is the day you announce the pre-order through publication and the following weeks.

In general, you want to have something new and exciting to say about your book. During the launch period, you have more things that you can say. How you announce these items is up to you, but here are the many things you can say during your launch period.

- ❒ Title Announcement
- ❒ Cover Announcement (can be the same as your pre-order announcement)
- ❒ ARC Sign-Up
- ❒ Pre-Order Announcement
- ❒ Initial rankings
- ❒ Early reader reviews/blurbs/editorial reviews
- ❒ Book unboxing
- ❒ Reminders ahead of launch (e.g., countdown posts)
- ❒ Review post reminder on publication day
- ❒ Review post reminder and final thank you **+2 days after publication**
- ❒ Celebration planning for launch day
- ❒ Launch party (can be you and your cat or a formal event at a bookstore)

WHERE THE READERS ARE

Now that you are getting the word out on your social media, you next need to go where the readers are. Not everyone on the internet likes to read. But there are specific corners of the internet that are chock full of readers, and that's where we want to be as authors. New platforms for book lovers are popping up all the time. I tend to be on the slow side of adoption. I'll sign up if a new platform for book lovers sticks around. But I tend to wait because I don't have time to sign up and manage every conceivable login. I have more books to write. Be judicious in adding more platforms for yourself as well.

Amazon Author Central Profile

https://author.amazon.com/

This isn't a social platform. But it is IMPERATIVE that you have your Amazon Author Central Account set up. When someone gets to your book page, they can click on your author name at the top of the page. If you don't have an Author Central profile set up, it will take them to a search results page which may or may not show all of your books. When your Author Central profile is active, it will take them to this profile, where all your books are easily listed. Also, you will want to leverage Author Central to put in any requests for updated categories or corrections on your book page.

- ☐ **Claim account.** Use the same login that you have for Amazon KDP.
- ☐ **Add bio and headshot**.
- ☐ Claim your book (***for first-time authors, you cannot do this until the book is up on Amazon.com).***
- ☐ Request all your categories (Page 174)
- ☐ Add an RSS feed with your blog content to update this page.
- ☐ Invite your audience to follow this page for new books and release updates.

A+ Content on Amazon.com Book Retail Page

If you elected to use Amazon KDP to self-publish your books to Amazon.com, this is an option for your book. If you did not, then move to the next topic.

A+ Content is now available to self-publishing authors. Search for almost any traditionally published book on Amazon.com, and you will see a "From The Publisher" section about halfway down the page. This usually contains additional reviews, praise for the book, graphics, or promotional images.

You can add this too. The possibilities are endless. You can show images of what the interior looks like – very helpful for children's books or cooking books. You can highlight the benefits of what you'll learn – an excellent addition for nonfiction books. You can use images to convey the feelings or emotions the characters will feel.

You can access this from the "Marketing" tab of your Amazon KDP dashboard.

Remember, this is something you can add on after the book is published, and you can optimize it or change it over time.

Goodreads

https://www.goodreads.com/

While there are new platforms like Goodreads on the market, this is currently the largest book community online. Here readers can add books to their "want to read" list and rate the books they have read. The algorithm recommends new books to them based on their ratings. You want your book here so people can easily find, share, and rate it.

- ❏ *Claim account.*
- ❏ *Add bio and headshot*.
- ❏ Claim your book (***for first-time authors, you cannot do this until the book is available for sale or pre-order).***
  - ○ Add cover.
  - ○ Add book description.
  - ○ Mark your book as "currently reading" – you can post status updates as the launch gets closer and post a review with pre-order or purchase links.
- ❏ Invite your audience to follow this page for new books and release updates.

- ☐ Research Goodreads Giveaways as a potential marketing option for your book.
- ☐ Join groups for authors and readers in your genre. Connect with readers and authors.

BookBub

https://partners.bookbub.com/authors/

BookBub is similar to Goodreads in that readers can follow authors, list books they want to read, and rate books they have already read. However, BookBub has a daily newsletter that goes out to book lovers. Getting your book listed in this newsletter is very competitive and pricey. Asking BookBub users to follow you and rate your books is free. But first, you need a profile for them to follow.

- ☐ ***Claim account.***
- ☐ ***Add bio and headshot***.
- ☐ Claim your book (****for first-time authors, you cannot do this until the book is available for sale or pre-order***).
- ☐ Invite your audience to follow this page for new books and release updates.
- ☐ Research BookBub Daily Deals and Paid Ads.

Podcasts Sell Books

Whether you write fiction or non-fiction, podcast interviews sell books. People who listen to podcasts want to be entertained and informed. They are usually also avid readers (or at least listen to audiobooks). Landing an interview or mention on a large podcast can help a whole new audience learn about your book.

Podcast hosts need to create new quality content for their audience on a regular basis. They are looking for things to talk about. But you can't just reach out and say, "hey, promote my book for me." You have to provide value to that audience and tell the host why you will make for an interesting guest.

Here are the steps you'll need to take to find and pitch podcasts:

- ☐ Listen to podcasts! The more you listen, the more you'll get a sense for how interviews flow.
- ☐ Compile a list of podcasts relevant to your topic or life experience.

- ❑ Listen to the podcasts you plan to pitch.
  - ○ Confirm they actually do interviews.
  - ○ Get a feel for whether you would even like talking to the host.
- ❑ **Craft a custom pitch for each podcast. Include up to three topics you can speak to that will add value to the audience.**
- ❑ Send the pitch and wait.
- ❑ Follow up once. (NOT DAILY!!)
- ❑ Respond to any interview requests.
- ❑ Prepare for your interview:
  - ○ Have the correct gear: microphone and headphones.
  - ○ Find a quiet space with minimal distractions.
  - ○ If it is also a video podcast, make sure you have a camera and subtly place your book in the background of the frame.
- ❑ Record and thank the host for their time.
- ❑ Promote the interview when it is live.

There is a lot of nuance here, and I have a free (no cost to you at all) email course where I can walk you through these steps at **AuthorYourAmbition.com/Courses**.

On the following pages, you'll find sheets where you can track your podcast research and pitch requests.

Podcast	Contact Info/ Host Name	Interviews on Podcast? (Y/N)	Topics I could cover that relate...	Pitch Sent (Y/N + Date Sent)	Response (Y/N)	Interview Date

Podcast	Contact Info/ Host Name	Interviews on Podcast? (Y/N)	Topics I could cover that relate...	Pitch Sent (Y/N + Date Sent)	Response (Y/N)	Interview Date

Podcast	Contact Info/ Host Name	Interviews on Podcast? (Y/N)	Topics I could cover that relate...	Pitch Sent (Y/N + Date Sent)	Response (Y/N)	Interview Date

BOOK INFLUENCERS

In the past few years, there has been an exciting new trend in book-selling: social media! Small (and large) scale book influencers can push backlist books back into the bestseller list. Beautiful photos, clever short and long-form videos, and book lovers' recommendations have helped sell lots of books! (This is why a beautiful cover is so critical – it has to LOOK good!)

Many of the more prominent influencers on BookStagram, BookTok, and BookTube receive advance copies of books from traditional publishers. They get these books for free and are sometimes compensated for their time reading and posting content. They usually run these accounts as a fun hobby. It isn't their full-time job. So, when you go and ask them to read and promote your book, you are one of many requests they field daily.

Here are the steps you'll need to take to find and pitch book influencers:

- ❏ Look at BookStagram posts. Watch BookTok and BookTube videos. Maybe create some of your own.
- ❏ Compile a list of influencers who highlight books in your genre. Whose aesthetic do you like?
- ❏ Follow and like their content.
- ❏ Craft a custom pitch to each creator.
- ❏ Send the pitch and wait.
- ❏ Follow up once. (NOT DAILY!!)
- ❏ Respond to any requests for the book. (**NOTE**: They will likely want a physical copy.)
- ❏ Share the posts when they promote your book.

On the following pages, you'll find sheets where you can track your influencer research and pitch requests.

Creator Handle	Platforms	Following on Social Media?	Book submission requirements for their channel?	Pitch Sent (Y/N + Date Sent)	Response (Y/N)	Book Sent Date	Book Received (Y/N)	Post Up on Social
	☐ BookStagram ☐ BookTok ☐ BookTube							
	☐ BookStagram ☐ BookTok ☐ BookTube							
	☐ BookStagram ☐ BookTok ☐ BookTube							

Creator Handle	Platforms	Following on Social Media?	Book submission requirements for their channel?	Pitch Sent (Y/N + Date Sent)	Response (Y/N)	Book Sent Date	Book Received (Y/N)	Post Up on Social
	☐ BookStagram ☐ BookTok ☐ BookTube							
	☐ BookStagram ☐ BookTok ☐ BookTube							
	☐ BookStagram ☐ BookTok ☐ BookTube							

Creator Handle	Platforms	Following on Social Media?	Book submission requirements for their channel?	Pitch Sent (Y/N + Date Sent)	Response (Y/N)	Book Sent Date	Book Received (Y/N)	Post Up on Social
	☐ BookStagram ☐ BookTok ☐ BookTube							
	☐ BookStagram ☐ BookTok ☐ BookTube							
	☐ BookStagram ☐ BookTok ☐ BookTube							

PAID ADVERTISING

I have put this section towards the end because I firmly believe that if you do not have your unpaid marketing together, no amount of paid advertising will help. If anything, it will only amplify the issues you are experiencing with sales and reviews (or lack thereof).

Work through these exercises if you have your organic marketing together and want to try advertising.

Here are a few terms to keep in mind:

Cost-Per-Click (CPC) or Pay-Per-Click (PPC) – Most of your advertising options with Amazon, BookBub, or Google are cost-per-click. Your ad will run, and many people will see it, but you will only pay when they click on it. (An ad that charges for views or impressions is on a CPM basis). In general, CPC is great. If you have good ad copy, you get lots of clicks, but if your ad copy isn't appealing, you don't get clicks, and you don't lose any money. You know what you have to tweak. You see what is effective and what you can tweak to optimize performance over time.

Cost-Per-Acquisition (CPA) – Some ads may charge a cost-per-acquisition, which is the best option. You only pay when you make a sale. But it can be hard to track this. You will likely calculate this on the back end. After paying for so many clicks, you will get a sale. How much did you spend to get that one sale? That is your CPA. If it is more than your royalty, then you are losing money on that sale. It can take some time to optimize or fine-tune, so a high CPA to start is okay, but you want to see it trending lower.

Return on Ad Spend (ROAS) – This is your ROI. How profitable are these ads? Are you breaking even? Are you spending multiples of your royalty on one sale? You may be able to tolerate a poor ROAS if you are starting and optimizing or trying to get people to start your series. But a poor ROAS means you are not earning back what you spend on ads.

In the beginning, look at your ad spend as money you will never see again. It is a learning period for the first couple of months to see what is or is not working.

MONTHLY BUDGET FOR ADS: $ _____
(this can be for one platform or across all ad platforms)

Format	Royalty	Cost Per Acquisition	# Sales Needed to Break Even	# Sales Realized this Month	Keep Running Yes/No
eBook					
Paperback					
Hardcover					
Audiobook					

Before you begin an ad campaign:

- ❏ Does your book have any reviews yet?
  - ○ If no, is it on pre-order? (If you have no reviews and your book is live, wait until you have some to start your ads.)
  - ○ If yes, how many? _____ (Track if the sales from your ads eventually result in reviews. A poor ROAS can be overlooked for this benefit.)
- ❏ Have you optimized your book page? Does it look as appealing as it can be for a reader?
- ❏ Do you know which categories, keywords, and comp books you will target with your ad?
- ❏ What is your budget?
- ❏ What is your success metric for this campaign? When will you cut it off?

HIRING AN ADS MANAGER

If you already feel like you don't have the time or wherewithal to learn and manage your own ads, you can hire someone to help you.

Where to find a great ads manager: You should use several sources to find different ad managers to work with. Keep in mind that longer lists are harder to whittle down. We are currently looking at making a list of potential ad managers. We will whittle down next.

- ☐ Search for Ads and Marketing on Reedsy. Check the reviews and only connect with advertisers you like.
- ☐ Ask other indie authors for recommendations.

VETTING POTENTIAL AD MANAGERS

It is essential to ask questions at this stage. You will be able to whittle down your list quickly as you find out who is in and out of your price range, who has the experience to help, and who communicates with you. A few critical items to consider:

- What is the payment structure? Do they get paid a commission on each book sale? A flat fee each month? An hourly fee? Some hybrid?

- Are they familiar with advertising self-published books? (Managing ads for a Fortune 500 Company is VERY different.)

- What is their philosophy on when to optimize and how to evaluate the data coming in?

- How do they communicate? What questions are they asking you? Do you think you will mesh well?

MARKETING NOTES

Throughout the lifetime of your book, you will have to market and promote it. What works for you will not work for other authors, and vice versa. As you try new marketing techniques and strategies, take notes! Make an experiment out of it! See how many more sales or reviews you can get as you tweak your copy, try new images, or reach out to a different podcast network. Keep notes here and add more to your notebook, journal, online task manager, etc.

Marketing techniques that worked!:

_____

_____

_____

_____

_____

_____

Marketing techniques that made no difference:

_____

_____

_____

_____

_____

_____

_____

Marketing techniques that BOMBED! (How could I make this work next time? Or completely avoid in the future?):

_____

_____

_____

_____

_____

_____

_____

_____

_____

_____

_____

_____

_____

_____

_____

_____

_____

_____

_____

MORE MARKETING UNTIL THE END OF TIME

Your book is launched and out to the world. And while it seems like a good time to relax and watch your royalties roll in, I have some bad news. The marketing never ends. It is a delicate balance to write your next book and market your backlist, but it is part of the job.

It can seem daunting, though. You just gave your best ideas to promote the book to your launch. Your brain may feel a little like a deflated balloon. Take a rest, and believe me, the ideas will keep coming.

Keep track of these marketing ideas. No idea is too big or too small at this point. But you will start to see which ideas resonate the most with you, which will be the easiest to execute on, and which will be the most difficult or expensive.

Below are some ideas to get you started and room for you to add more:

❑ Reminder posts on social media for readers to leave a review. Promote positive reviews when they come in to encourage reviews and sales.

❑ Promote when a library picks up the book to encourage more library purchases.

❑ Engage with your local library and indie bookstores.

❑ Amazon Book Page Optimizations:

   ○ Claim author profile on Author Central
   ○ Add book to series (if applicable)
   ○ Add A+ content
   ○ Optimize book description every 90 days
   ○ Optimize keywords and categories as needed

❑ _____

❑ _____

❑ _____

- [ ] _____
- [ ] _____
- [ ] _____
- [ ] _____
- [ ] _____
- [ ] _____
- [ ] _____
- [ ] _____
- [ ] _____
- [ ] _____
- [ ] _____
- [ ] _____
- [ ] _____
- [ ] _____
- [ ] _____
- [ ] _____
- [ ] _____
- [ ] _____
- [ ] _____
- [ ] _____
- [ ] _____
- [ ] _____
- [ ] _____
- [ ] _____

THE NEXT BOOK!

There is a saying, "more books sell more books!" And this is true. When you have more books available for readers to choose from, it is easier for them to pick among your titles. Finishing a series can help sell more because there are three or four books (or more) to read through.

While this entire process may have been daunting, you likely have more ideas for books. And you'll be able to get back to why you started this whole endeavor: to write!

Here are some things to keep in mind when writing and promoting your next book:

- ❏ Start promoting right away – "I have a new idea..."
- ❏ Go through this workbook again. Check your strategy and optimize where you need to. You'll learn so much each time you publish.
- ❏ What has to be updated when the next book is on sale?
    - ○ **Website** – Update menu navigation with additional book pages as well as homepage cover images and your biography
    - ○ **Social Media** – Update header images and biography
    - ○ **Front matter of existing books** – Update – "works published" list
    - ○ **Back matter of existing books** – Update biography

> ▶ I have a video on how to update your backlist on my channel. Take some ideas from this, but your backlist marketing is as unique as your book and author brand.

ONGOING AUTHOR DEVELOPMENT

As you write each book, you can finetune and refine your process. But with more books, you'll have more of a business on your hands. As creators, we constantly evolve, and we need to keep learning. Here are my recommendations for how you can prioritize your ongoing development as an author:

Craft

What are my weaknesses?

_____

_____

_____

_____

What do I want to improve for my next book?

_____

_____

_____

_____

What books, courses, channels, and podcasts can help me?

_____

_____

_____

Author Business

What is the aim for my author business?

_____

_____

_____

_____

_____

What do I need to learn and build to get there?

_____

_____

_____

_____

_____

What books, courses, channels, and podcasts can help me?

_____

_____

_____

_____

_____

_____

_____

Professional Organizations

What organizations support authors who write in my genre?

_____

_____

_____

_____

_____

What organizations support experts in my field/topic?

_____

_____

_____

_____

_____

_____

What local author meet-ups or online masterminds are available to me?

_____

_____

_____

_____

I am a member of the Alliance of Independent Authors. After looking at all the potential organizations I could join, I picked this one. I support their message and enjoy the community they have built.

BIBLIOGRAPHY

Roberts, Dale L. *The Amazon Self-Publisher: How to Sell More Books on Amazon.* 2021.

Chesson, Dave. "How to Create a Professional Author Page in Amazon Author Central." Kindlepreneur Podcast. https://kindlepreneur.com/amazon-author-central-page/

"Complete BISAC Subject Headings List, 2021 Edition". BISG. https://bisg.org/page/BISACEdition

"Draft2Digital Partners" Draft2Digital. https://www.draft2digital.com/partners/

"Global Distribution with IngramSpark" IngramSpark. https://www.ingramspark.com/how-it-works/distribute

"LuLu Retail Distribution" LuLu. https://www.lulu.com/sell/retail-distribution

"PublishDrive Distribution Services" PublishDrive. https://publishdrive.com/book-distribution-services.html

"Findaway Voices: Selling Audiobooks" Findaway Voices. https://findawayvoices.com/selling-audiobooks

"ACX Audio Submission Requirements." ACX. https://www.acx.com/help/acx-audio-submission-requirements/201456300

RESOURCES

More questions? Schedule some time to connect with me directly or check out my YouTube Channel.

YouTube Channels

M.K. Williams: https://youtube.com/mkwilliamsauthor

Self-Publishing with Dale: https://www.youtube.com/selfpublishingwithdale

Keith Wheeler Books: https://www.youtube.com/c/keithwheelerbooks

Author Level-Up: https://www.youtube.com/c/AuthorLevelUp

Podcasts

The Creative Penn with Joanna Penn: https://podcasts.apple.com/gb/podcast/the-creative-penn-podcast-for-writers/id309426367

Alliance of Independent Authors: https://podcasts.apple.com/us/podcast/askalli-self-publishing-advice-podcast/id1080135033?mt=2

The Indy Author: https://www.theindyauthor.com/podcast.html

Podcasting for Authors: https://www.theindyauthor.com/podcasting-for-authors.html

Kindlepreneur Blog

Guide to Writing a Book Copyright Page: https://kindlepreneur.com/book-copyright-page-examples-ebook/

Social Media Groups

20BooksTo50K- https://www.facebook.com/groups/20Booksto50k

Wide for the Win- https://www.facebook.com/groups/556186621558858

IngramSpark Author Community- https://www.facebook.com/groups/641752356577267

KDP Print Templates:

https://kdp.amazon.com/en_US/help/topic/G201834230

IngramSpark Calculator:

https://myaccount.ingramspark.com/Portal/Tools/PubCompCalculator

IngramSpark Knowledge Base: https://help.ingramspark.com/hc/en-us

Copyright and Legal Items:

U.S. Copyright Office Online Registration Portal: https://www.copyright.gov/registration/

Helen Sedwick's *Self-Publisher's Legal Handbook: The Step-by-Step Guide to the Legal Issues of Self-Publishing*

"Guide to Writing a Book Copyright Page" *Kindlepreneur.* July 20, 2021: https://kindlepreneur.com/book-copyright-page-examples-ebook/

"DMCA Email Templates" *Scribd Help Center.* https://support.scribd.com/hc/en-us/articles/210128926-DMCA-email-templates

Services:

Reedsy: https://reedsy.com/r/m-k-williams

Grammarly: https://grammarly.go2cloud.org/SH2QA

Formatted Books: https://formattedbooks.com/?ref=31

100 Covers: http://100covers.com/?ref=49

BookBrush https://bookbrush.com/

Books2Read:

https://books2read.com/links/ubl/create/

Advertising Platforms for Authors:

Amazon Advertising: https://advertising.amazon.com/

BookBub: https://partners.bookbub.com/ads

NEED MORE HELP?

My aim with this workbook was to help you. If you still feel that you need more help, please check out these additional resources I have put together:

- ❐ Check out my YouTube videos and tutorials. Channel members get access to an exclusive monthly video and Q&As.
- ❐ Subscribe for a discount on my collection of Author Your Ambition books aimed at helping first-time authors.
- ❐ Schedule a 1-on-1 call with me. I usually have one or two openings a month, and we can review a personalized plan for your book.

ACKNOWLEDGMENTS

This checklist only exists because you, the reader, exist. Because of the many questions I once had when starting this journey. Because of the same questions many authors have asked me over the years. This checklist would not exist in this form without you. I envisioned you this entire time, the excitement and ambition, the questions and the anxiety. I hope you finish this and have your own book in hand. I hope your words find their intended audience and change the world.

None of this could have happened without one man: Jason Williams. He is the one who first encouraged me to self-publish. Who challenged me and cheered me on each step of the way. Who read the least coherent and comma-free version of this workbook. He constantly champions my work while reminding me to take a break. Without Jason Williams, there is no author M.K. Williams and no Author Your Ambition. Thank you, Jason!

Next, I want to thank my ever-patient Beta-Readers. They are all authors. Some write fiction, some non-fiction. Some have a handful of books published, others just one. Some have a dream for a book in their hearts. They all combed through this book to point out what wasn't clear. In the years I have been writing and self-publishing, I have forgotten some of the first-timer questions. These amazing Beta Readers brought their corrections and perspective and made this a better checklist for every author moving forward. Thank you to Kyle Landis-Marinello, Doug Nordman, Estelle van de Velde, S.D. Huston, Jessica Wason, and Monica Scudieri

Next, I want to thank the Author Your Ambition Community. Every week I post a new video on my YouTube channel. By some miracle, authors find those videos and ask questions. They follow up for clarification. They post their wins and challenges. This is the community I work so hard for. To be there for them. Because I didn't have a community like that when I was starting. I wouldn't have new videos, questions to answer, or a workbook like this to put together without these fantastic authors.

Check out other books in the Author Your Ambition Series:

**Self-Publishing for the
First-Time Author**

**Book Marketing for the
First-Time Author**

**How to Write Your First Novel:
A Guide for Aspiring
Fiction Authors**

**Going Wide:
Self-Publishing Your Books
Outside the Amazon Ecosystem**

AUTHOR BIO

M.K. Williams is an author and independent publisher. She left her career in sports marketing to pursue writing and publishing full-time in 2019. Williams has published multiple novels and non-fiction guides. In addition to publishing her own works, she has helped established companies bring their information to the masses by publishing books under their brands. She focuses on helping aspiring authors realize their dreams. When she isn't writing, she enjoys running and reading in her spare time.

Lightning Source UK Ltd.
Milton Keynes UK
UKHW051228050123
414849UK00025B/211